War in European History

MICHAEL HOWARD

War in European History

OXFORD UNIVERSITY PRESS

LONDON OXFORD NEW YORK

1976

Oxford University Press

OXFORD LONDON NEW YORK
GLASGOW TORONTO MELBOURNE WELLINGTON
CAPE TOWN IBADAN NAIROBI DAR ES SALAAM LUSAKA ADDIS ABABA
DELHI BOMBAY CALCUTTA MADRAS KARACHI LAHORE DACCA
KUALA LUMPUR SINGAPORE HONG KONG TOKYO

Paperback ISBN 0 19 289095 6
Casebound ISBN 0 19 211564 2

© Oxford University Press 1976

First published in the Oxford Paperbacks University Series (1976) and simultaneously in a cloth bound edition.

Howard, Michael
War in European History

ISBN 0–19–211564–2
ISBN 0–19–289095–6 Pbk
ITI
DCG 40
LCD 25
LCSH European-History

Set in Great Britain by Gloucester Typesetting Co Ltd
Printed by Fletcher & Son Ltd, Norwich

FOR MARK AND ERIC

Contents

Foreword

The Editor of the OPUS series invited me to write this
work as a successor to Professor Cyril Falls's *The Art of War
from the Age of Napoleon to the Present Day*, which the Oxford
University Press published for the Home University Library
in 1961. But Professor Falls's study is an inimitable gem of
learning and exposition which leaves very little more to be
said on the subjects that he covered. It seemed best therefore to
expand the subject matter both chronologically and in scope:
to study not simply 'the Art of War' but the institution of
warfare as it has developed within European society over the
millenium for which we have reliable records, and to attempt
to trace, not simply the development of warfare itself, but its
connection with, and effect on, technical, social and economic
change throughout this period.

Until comparatively recently the study of war has been
didactic and normative: that is, the wars of the past were
studied in order to deduce either immutable principles or
lines of development as guides to the efficient conduct of war
in the future. So long as the organized use, or threatened use,
of force still remains an instrument in the conduct of international relations, such analytic studies will continue to be
needed, and Professor Falls's work will rank high among them.
But to abstract war from the environment in which it is fought
and study its technique as one would those of a game is to
ignore a dimension essential to the understanding, not simply
of the wars themselves but of the societies which fought them.
The historian who studies war, not to develop norms for action
but to enlarge his understanding of the past, cannot be simply
a 'military historian', for there is literally no branch of human

activity which is not to a greater or lesser extent relevant to his subject. He has to study war not only, as Hans Delbrück put it, in the framework of political history, but in the framework of economic, social and cultural history as well. War has been part of a totality of human experience, the parts of which can be understood only in relation to one another. One cannot adequately describe how wars were fought without giving some idea of what they were fought about.

There are now numerous books which take this philosophy as the basis for their approach to the history of war, and I have done little more than put together in a very superficial fashion some of the ideas I have gleaned from them. A list will be found in the bibliographical note at the end of this work. I have also benefited greatly from discussions with my colleagues Professors J. M. Wallace-Hadrill and Lionel Butler, who tactfully punctured some of my more ridiculous misconceptions about the Middle Ages, and Professor S. E. Finer, whose insights into the place of armed forces in modern societies have been most valuable. I am particularly grateful to the Vice-Chancellor, faculty and students of the University of Warwick, who not only allowed me to try out some of my ideas on them in the Radcliffe Lectures in the Spring Term of 1975, but actually paid me to do so.

All Souls College, Oxford   MICHAEL HOWARD
November 1975

I

The Wars of the Knights

'The origins of Europe', a historian of the Middle Ages has recently reminded us 'were hammered out on the anvil of war';[1] and indeed 'war' is really too benign a term to describe the condition of the European continent once the precarious Pax Romana had disintegrated and waves of invaders swept over it; Goths and Vandals from the east, Moslems from the south and finally, most terrible of all, Vikings from the north. Nearly six hundred years elapsed between the first barbarian incursions in the fourth century and the end of the tenth century, when the last of the invaders had been either assimilated or repulsed. Then in their turn the peoples of Europe began to expand, first eastward and then, as they learned the arts of navigation, southward and westward. So for a time-span as long as that which divides the thirteenth century from our own day, 'peace' in Europe, that peace for which the congregations in Christian churches so sincerely prayed, existed only in exceptional and precarious oases of time and place. It is hardly surprising that an entire social pattern should have come into being to enable the peoples of Europe to survive in such an environment: the pattern to be known to later generations of historians as 'feudalism'.

The successive quasi-nomadic warrior societies followed, clashed with, and absorbed one another like the waves of a turbulent sea. Following the Gothic and other invaders of the fourth century came those Frankish tribes who, loosely associated under the leadership of the Merovingian family, were to repulse the Moslems invading France from the south in the eighth century and to create, under the Carolingians at the beginning of the ninth, the short-lived unity of the west. The lands east of the Rhine had then to face for nearly a hundred years the onslaughts of the Magyars. For an even longer period the coastal districts of northern, western and southern Europe —and inland regions as far as long-boats could penetrate upstream—were ravaged by Vikings from Scandinavia; looting, burning, sometimes settling. Such a settlement was made in Normandy at the beginning of the tenth century. Then for two centuries the Normans, Christianized, feudalized, the acknowledged warrior-leaders of Europe, extended their own sway; conquering the Saxon kingdom of England and the Moslems in south Italy and Sicily; and finally, at the end of the eleventh century, turning the tide of invasion back from Europe and beginning to penetrate into Asia in their turn with the First Crusade. Simultaneously, in the same holy cause, the warrior-caste in Germany, having sealed up the Magyars in Hungary, began to push their own frontiers eastward again, subduing, colonizing, and converting the heathen Slavs.

'Feudalism' was a response to economic as much as to military necessity. The decline of economic activity resulting from the Moslem disruption of the historic Mediterranean trading area meant that by the beginning of the ninth century specie was rare in Europe and land the only source of wealth. Further, the variety of threats that the Carolingians had to meet made mobility in their forces essential—mobility to match that given the Vikings by their long-boats, the Magyars by their tough little ponies. This could be provided only by the horse. And once the stirrup came into general use among the Franks, in the eighth century, the horse could be used not simply for mobility but for fighting.[2] Speed could be converted into shock. Spears need no longer be thrown but could be couched as lances and rammed home. Horsemen thus armed had an advantage over men fighting on foot as absolute as that which, a millenium later, men armed with breech-loading firearms had over enemies armed only with spears. And in both cases military dominance was to lead to political control.

So during the eighth and ninth centuries the only fighting man of any consequence, the only *miles* who counted, was the

mounted warrior, the knight.* In 866 Charlemagne's grandson
Charles the Bald summoning his tenants-in-chief to the feudal
host, insisted that they should attend mounted, and ever
thereafter they did. So there began a process of expensive
escalation all too familiar in our own day. In a clash between
mounted forces—as later in tank or in naval warfare—
advantage came from a combination of range, protection, and
speed. Range came from longer and thus heavier lances.
Protection was provided by armour. In the first instance this
consisted of a coat of mail reaching from neck to knee; itself an
expensive item of equipment and, after the horse itself, the
knight's most valuable possession. Speed had to be balanced,
in the horse, against the weight necessary to bear an increasingly heavy load; so horses were specially bred for their
carrying and staying power and the momentum they could
engender in the charge. For an extended campaign, more than
one such horse was necessary, and anyhow the knight needed
help in manipulating and carrying his growing impedimenta
—lance, battle-sword, helmet, shield. At the very least he
needed a shield-bearer, *escuyer*, esquire; probably a groom as
well; a more lightly mounted horseman to scout and skirmish
for him; and one or two foot soldiers to stand guard. So the
single knight expanded into a 'lance', a team of half a dozen
men, like the crew of some enormous battle tank. The whole
apparatus came very expensive indeed.

The management of these heavy weapons and horses in
armoured combat was no matter for amateurs; nor could
expensive forces of this kind be easily found from a subsistence
economy. By the tenth century war was becoming a business
for wealthy specialists who trained for it from early youth.
How could they be provided with the economic security to
enable them to devote themselves to their expertise? Primarily
by grants of land, in return for which they pledged service and
'allegiance' to their lord. This grant was the 'fief' that lay at
the basis of feudal society: a threefold relationship of military
specialization, land tenure, and personal obligation, whereby

* It is curious that whereas the French word *chevalier* and German *Ritter*
translate the meaning exactly, the English have simply a word which in modern
German (*Knecht*) means 'retainer' or 'groom'.

a landholding warrior class developed free of all duties save that of rendering mounted service to their lord for a given number of days during the year. To assure possession of their land they built themselves castles. These were normally sited so as to command access roads, with a 'donjon' or keep in which their family could live, outbuildings for their retainers, the whole surrounded by a high curtain wall rendered proof by battlements against escalade and protected by a moat. Medieval castles were symbols of effective power, and wars tended to consist of straightforward struggles for their possession.

The descendants of that warrior class—a few hundred families constantly intermarrying and as constantly reinforced by fresh recruits—were to retain the landed dominance of Europe until the sixteenth century, political dominance until the eighteenth, and traces at least of social dominance until our own day. 'To bear arms', to have a crest on one's helmet and symbols on one's shield instantly recognizable in the heat of battle, became in European society for a thousand years a symbol of nobility. For what it is worth it still is. But in the Middle Ages it was a symbol of *function* and available to all who performed that function. The nobility was not yet a close hereditary caste; war was still a career open to the talents.

But having achieved nobility through military prowess, the man-at-arms was expected to comport himself according to a certain code of conduct. Very rapidly the warrior function became enhanced with a dimension of semi-numinous ceremony. Much of the 'Middle Ages' is still seen through the distorting lenses of fifteenth century legend, which cast upon the whole world of 'chivalry' a golden and fictitious glamour, a sunset glow from a consciously disappearing society.[3] But the concept of 'chivalry' itself, which was in essence simply the behaviour of *chevaliers* or knights, was certainly older—as old at least as the troubadours whose poetry in the dawn of European literature in the twelfth century hymned the virtues not only of courage but of honour, gentleness, courtesy and, by and large, chastity. The chevalier had to be not only *sans peur* but *sans reproche*. Knighthood was a way of life, sanctioned and civilized by the ceremonies of the Church until it was almost indistinguishable from the ecclesiastical orders of the monasteries. Indeed in the twelfth century military orders—the Templars, the Knights of St. John, the Teutonic Knights—were established in conscious imitation of the monastic foundations. The sword-belt and spurs set the knight apart as distinctively as the tonsure did the monk and the priest; and in the mythical figures of Parsifal and Galahad priest and knight became indistinguishable, equally dedicated, equally holy, the ideal to which medieval Christendom aspired.

This remarkable blend of Germanic warrior and Latin *sacerdos* lay at the root of all medieval culture. The Church accepted and blessed the warrior class from the very beginning: since they were fighting to defend Christendom against the incursions of heathen Moslems, Magyars, and Norsemen, it could hardly do otherwise. Its members—bishops, abbots—happily assumed military obligations with the fiefs of land granted them by the kings they crowned, and seldom showed much reluctance about bearing arms so long as they did not actually shed blood: something seldom done by that useful weapon, the mace. At the same time they made attempts, increasingly successfully as the barbarian incursions ebbed, to bring the conduct of war and Christian morality into some kind of focus. Concepts of *jus ad bellum* and *jus in bello* had little relevance when the Norsemen were raging through the land like devouring flames, and churchmen found as much difficulty in applying them to Moslems who were themselves fanatically determined to convert or to extirpate the infidel wherever their swords could reach him. So in war against the pagan no holds were barred, and knights indeed could gain remission from their sins by waging it. In the twelfth century the Teutonic Knights were, under the auspices of the Church, to conduct against the Slavs and Wends in eastern Europe a crusade which was virtually a war of extermination.

Within Christendom however the situation was, at least in principle, different. That Christians should fight one another was deplorable and the Church deplored it as regularly and as ineffectively then as it has done ever since. But Christian theologians agreed that certain wars were 'just'; broadly speaking, those waged on the authority of a lawful superior in a righteous cause. And it was not surprising that a class of men brought up for generations for fighting, when an external adversary was lacking (and even when he was not) should fight one another. In the absence of any commonly accepted authority with the power to enforce its judgements, armed conflict would have been probable in a far less bellicose community. The web of rights and obligations, of duties and allegiances involved by feudal tenure gave rise to endless disputes, and in default of a clear system of law and law enforcement, men were likely to vindicate their rights by battle.

Such battle was seen as an appeal to God's judgement, and for the greater part of the Middle Ages every man of honour had the right to wage it. Only gradually was a distinction made, under the influence of Roman Law concepts, between 'private war' between individuals and 'public war' conducted by princes, and only gradually did the former category become outlawed. It was accepted that 'private war', *guerre couverte*, should be waged with as little damage as possible to the general community: a man might kill his adversary in battle, but not burn or despoil his property. In 'public war' the limits were broader. Prisoners could be taken and held to ransom; the property of the enemy was lawful booty; contributions could be levied on the population. In principle not only ecclesiastics and their possessions but the tillers of the soil were exempt from looting and pillage. But that exemption did not apply if they were suspected of giving 'aid and countenance' to the war, which they usually were. Finally there was a yet more terrible form of war, at its most common in siege warfare when the besieged fortress refused to surrender when summoned: *guerre mortelle*, in which not only the property but the lives of the vanquished were at the mercy of the conqueror.

By the fourteenth century the laws and limitations on the conduct of war were elaborate, much written about, and fairly uniform throughout western Christendom. They derived partly from the pressure of the Church, partly from the growing influence of Roman Law and partly from the codification of practice over centuries carried out by those indispensable experts, the lawyers of chivalry, the Heralds. They were enforced by courts of honour throughout Europe; they were seen less as a system of positive law or as restraints consciously dictated by humanitarianism than as a code of social behaviour. This was what was 'done' or 'not done' between knights. Under some circumstances butchery of prisoners was permissible (if a declaration of *guerre mortelle* was made by word or sign at the beginning of a battle) and under others, not: it was not considered to be wrong in itself, any more than women and children were seen as possessing *eo ipso* any kind of privileged immunity. If they were part of the garrison of a fortress which was taken by storm after rejecting a summons to surrender, they were put to the sword, and responsibility for their death lay squarely with the commander who, by failing to yield when summoned, brought their fate down on them.

But the increasing codification of the laws of war was due less to any searching of Christian, legal, or knightly consciences than to a very different development indeed: the growing commercialization of war.[4] Ransom and booty were no longer agreeable bonuses but, for a growing number of belligerents, the major object of their activity. The pay for which men enlisted was always exiguous, but the profits of a campaign might make their fortunes. So it was important to know, if war was to be conducted and peace concluded in an orderly manner, what and when booty could be seized and how it should be divided; what ransom could be asked, and who could legitimately ask it. Expectation of these legitimate rewards for services obediently rendered, risks courageously courted, and trials patiently undergone was, by the end of the Middle Ages, the motive which led men to set out on a campaign. Even within a framework of strict feudalism war could be a thoroughly mercenary occupation for all classes of society.

In any case, as medieval historians are constantly at pains to remind us, feudalism was neither uniform nor exclusive of other systems of tenure and service in Europe. It might be helpful to look at some of its variations.

In France, where the systems originated, the inability of the later Carolingians to provide more than the semblance of protection for their lands against the Norsemen led to the decentralization of effective power on to allegedly subordinate 'counts' (the *comites*, 'companions' of the old Germanic warrior bands), who settled in hereditary and so virtually independent fiefs such as Hainault, Flanders, Brittany, Provence; increasingly neglectful of the obligations they owed a Crown in no position to enforce them. For its own protection the Crown had to fall back whenever it could, not only on the knights of its own household, but on stipendiary troops, *soldi*, soldiers. These might be landless knights at a loose end—an increasing number as peace in Europe was gradually established and its population began to grow; or mounted troops more economically equipped than knights, known as *servientes*, or sergeants; or foot soldiers contemptuously—or perhaps convivially?—called *fanti*, boys; or the expensive specialists in that miracle of twelfth-century technology, the cross-bow, who had usually to be imported from Italy or Provence.

All this required money; but with the economic recovery of the twelfth century money was becoming more generally available in the hands of merchants and ecclesiastics, and even of certain members of the nobility who were acquiring bourgeois habits and preferred to pay cash—'scutage'—in lieu of military service. So by the beginning of the thirteenth century the King of France, Philip Augustus, was able to deploy a considerable standing army against his Angevin cousin John, King of England; whose efforts to increase his own independent military potential by extending his royal powers of jurisdiction and taxation brought him to grief at the hands, not of Philip, but of his own barons at Runnymede.

In southern Europe the position was a great deal more complex: partly because of the continuous warfare against the Moslems in Spain and southern Italy, partly because in the Mediterranean area a money economy never entirely disappeared and revived sooner than anywhere else. Knights therefore were both more independent and more mercenary. Those in southern France had their own strongholds and acknowledged no overlord. The arrogant independence of the Castilian nobility (the very name of whose land—the country of castles—is expressive) was notorious even in medieval Europe. In Catalonia, with its easier communications, the Counts of Barcelona were able more effectively to impose subordination on their more distant vassals and, aided by a fanatically militant church, pushed on with the *reconquista* of central and southern Spain from the Moslems at a steadier and more rapid pace.

In Italy urban communities survived among the rural *noblesse*, impervious to the feudalism spread by the Carolingians from Lombardy in the north and later by the Normans from the south; and merchants and landowners, townsmen and peasant, all without discrimination bore arms when threatened by Magyar raids from the north and Moslem raids from the sea. Military service was general. Cities were defended by their own citizen militias. As elsewhere, status was determined by armament, but in Italy armament was determined not so much by tenure as by wealth.

By the twelfth century the raiders had been repulsed from the Italian peninsula for good, except for the Normans who had imposed their stern and effective rule in Sicily and southern Italy. But the military habits of five hundred years died hard. The conflict between Pope and Emperor at the end of the eleventh century polarized Italian society in a continuing feud which divided city against city, family against family, in a civil war which provided a paradise for the free-lance soldier of fortune without, providentially, inhibiting the economic growth which made it possible for his employers to go on paying him.

In Germany in the Rhine valley feudalism developed as intensively as it did in northern France, and the mystique of *Rittertum*, knighthood, was as strong as anywhere in Europe. But further east tenure by military service was introduced more slowly, as was mounted warfare. Like their ancestors of Tacitus's day the German tribes of Saxony and Franconia and Swabia remained a free peasantry fighting on foot with axe and spear until, in the tenth century, there came the shock of the Magyar raids; hordes of mounted archers sweeping westward across the plains of northern Germany. Belatedly the Germans caught up with their cousins to the west, developed a cavalry force and the social system to support it and won, under Henry and Otto of Saxony, those victories at Merseburg in 933 and the Lerchfeld in 955 which established the Ottonian dynasty as the successors of the Carolingians and won for Otto himself the Imperial Crown. Some of the new feudal *noblesse* thereafter followed their Imperial lords into their disastrous adventures in Italy. Others joined the new crusading order, the Teutonic Knights, and sought adventure and lands and salvation of their souls to the east, among the plains and forests of Courland and Poland and Prussia, where their rapine and slaughter was sanctified by an indulgent Church. There they established themselves as a dominant class which was to be heard of again in European history.

As for England, the Norse invasions of the ninth and tenth centuries led the Saxon kings to supplement the *fyrd*, the obligation of all free men to bear arms, with a system of tenure somewhat on the lines of their Carolingian contemporaries across the Channel. But it was the Norman conquest, which placed all land at the disposal of the Crown, that made possible a system of feudal tenure and obligation as complete as anywhere in Europe. The Norman kings replaced the Saxon thegns by their own tenants in chief who, to carry out their task as an occupation-force in hostile territory, built the great castles which survive till our own time.

But militarily speaking the Norman dynasty in England and their successors were hopelessly overstretched; not only keeping the native English in order and extending their frontiers into Scotland and Wales, but maintaining their own rights on the mainland of Europe. Obligatory service from tenants-in-chief—*servitium debitum*—formed the nucleus of Norman and, later, Angevin armies in the eleventh and twelfth centuries; but the sixty days of which it customarily consisted was never enough to assemble a force and get it over to fight on the Continent, let alone to reduce the rebellious Scottish and Welsh mountaineers to obedience. Feudalism, in short, was not enough. The kings of England had to improvise. They hired freelances from the continent. They expanded their own military households. They tightened up on feudal obligation by 'distraint of knighthood' and then permitted those liable for service to commute their obligations for cash payments with which to hire mercenaries. They made contacts—'indentures' —with their own vassals for the provision of forces against cash payment; and, especially for wars within the island itself, they levied foot soldiers from among the local population by 'commission of array'.

Foot soldiers; among them, archers, whose value had been shown in the guerilla campaigns with which Edward I had to contend in the Welsh mountains at the end of the thirteenth century. In such warfare the heavy cavalry of the feudal host was of little value on its own. These knights were trained to fight their own kind, and in so doing to sweep unprotected infantry from the open ground where their mounted opponents normally chose to give battle. But in Wales they came up against an adversary who was not a military aristocracy like themselves, nor a conquering tribe to be chased back to its own lands, but men defending their own mountains; men who skilfully harassed them but seldom stood to fight. It was more like hunting game than war between Christians: foot soldiers were needed as beaters to flush the Welshmen out of their cover, long-bowmen to bring them down with long shots at distant or fleeting targets. And these long-bowmen proved their worth also in pitched battle in the traditional rôle of *artillery*, delivering missile fire to disorganize the enemy ranks before the charging knights delivered the *coup de grâce*; techniques used to good effect in the wars against the Scots early in the fourteenth century. This had been since the twelfth century the rôle of the cross-bowmen; but for every bolt discharged by the cross-bow, the long-bow with its six-foot shaft could get off five or six arrows, which by the end of the fourteenth century were lethal at 400 yards; without the destructive effect of the cross-bow bolt, admittedly, but still able to pierce chain mail.

So, anyhow, it was discovered at the remarkable battle of Creçy in 1346. Edward III had invaded France seven years earlier to prosecute his claim to the French crown—one of those interminable succession problems which were to keep the military *noblesse* of Europe happily occupied for another four centuries—with an immensely expensive army consisting mainly of mercenary German princelings paid for by loans from the merchants of the Hanse. The King of France prudently avoided battle; Edward's allies drifted home as the money ran out and he had no credit to raise more. By the campaign of 1346 he had so few mounted knights left that, on encountering the greatly superior French host, he dismounted them and set them to fight, as they had learned to do in the Scottish wars, among the archers to encourage them to stand their ground. The remarkable thing about Creçy was not so much the havoc the long-bowmen caused to the French chivalry— more than 1500 *killed*, according to reliable authorities, for about a hundred English casualties[5]—but the fact that they remained to cause any havoc at all; instead of fleeing, as infantry normally did in medieval warfare, at the first onset of the enemy horse.

Creçy was not the first occasion on which the mounted feudal host had been worsted by foot soldiers. In 1302 the burghers of Courtrai had successfully stood their ground with pike and spear against the mounted knights of the Count of Flanders. But the humiliation of Creçy forced the French chivalry, the fashionable pacemakers of the western world, to reconsider their equipment and their tactics. They abandoned chain mail for plate armour—a material which anyhow lent itself far more readily to decorative ornamentation indicating wealth and status; and they also dismounted for battle. This they did partly because of the vulnerability of their horses; partly because of the growing expense of maintaining a force of fully-equipped 'lances'; but partly out of considerations of pure gallantry: a dismounted knight could not flee to save himself but had to stand and fight. So long as they *stood* and fought the French chivalry enjoyed some success. But when they attacked, their invulnerability to arrows was outweighed by their ponderousness of movement and restriction of vision, which enabled the English to notch up two further victories at Poitiers in 1356 and most notably in Agincourt in 1415; where the English killed probably *five thousand* Frenchmen (a thousand after they had taken them prisoner) for the loss of a few hundred men of their own.[6]

By the fifteenth century a 'man-at-arms' with all his equipment and servitors was thus proving both inefficient on the battlefield, and expensive to sustain. And as their usefulness diminished, so their pretensions grew. Their armour becoming impossibly ornate, their tournaments more costly, their social status more jealously hedged around by a heraldic lore which concentrated the more on questions of status as it had less to do with military function. New knightly orders were founded in conscious imitation of the great orders of the twelfth century: the Knights of the Garter, the Knights of the Bath, the Knights of the Golden Fleece were the decadent if decorative successors of the warriors of the Temple and St. John of Jerusalem and the great fighting orders of Spain. Most remarkable, all continued to think, doggedly, of the reconquest of Jerusalem—even as the advancing Ottoman Turks were prizing loose the last strongholds of the crusaders in the eastern Mediterranean and beginning to threaten their bases in the West. The reconquest of Jerusalem was indeed one of the misty objectives floating before the eyes of Charles VIII of France when he invaded Italy in 1494.

It was not the French chivalry who finally bundled the English back into their island, effective as the work of Joan of Arc no doubt was in rousing them. It was another professional group who enjoyed no social status whatever and were barely accorded even the humble status of soldiers: the gunners.

The use of some form of combustible material—'Greek fire' as it was loosely called—had long been used in warfare both by the Byzantine armies and the Moslems, normally in the form of fireballs propelled by catapult in siege or naval warfare. To reverse the process and use combustion itself as a propellant of missiles was a more difficult and dangerous affair, demanding among other things an expertise in metal casting which was developed in the West, ironically enough, to serve that most peaceful of purposes, bell founding. From bells to bombards was an all too easy step, and it appears to have been taken early in the fourteenth century. The first experiments—great mortars which could be fired only once a day, *ribauldequins* or bundles of tubes like primitive *mitrailleuses*, infernal machines lovingly moulded by medieval craftsmen in the shape of dragons and devils—are depicted, sometimes highly imaginatively, in the earliest printed books. By the fifteenth century the more exotic products had disappeared, and the two weapons which between them were to dominate the conduct of war for another five hundred years were emerging in clearly recognizable form: the cannon and the hand gun. Men complained as bitterly about them as today we do about napalm; not simply because they were inhumane in their effects but because they degraded war, putting as they did the noble man-at-arms at the mercy of the vile and base born. But as today, those who complained about the presence of these weapons in their opponents' armies regarded it as an unanswerable argument for providing them in their own.

Both weapons were integrated into the revived French armies of the fifteenth century and used effectively against an England where a combination of military nostalgia and political confusion held back any comparable innovations. On the battlefield a few artillery discharges at the beginning shattered the ranks of the archers and enabled the men-at-arms to close for hand-to-hand fighting on equal terms. More generally the kings of France developed a train of siege artillery before which the castles protecting the lands of the English crown in France crumbled into heaps of stones. The English military dominance which characterized Europe at the end of the fourteenth century had fifty years later completely disappeared; and the archers of Creçy and Agincourt were looked on as a historical curiosity.

The future was to lie with foot soldiers of another kind. The simplest weapon with which a man on foot can be armed against cavalry is a spear; and if the spears are long enough, and the ranks are dense enough, and the morale of the men is high enough, such a formation can be almost invincible unless it can be broken up by some kind of bombardment. The Macedonian phalanx, after all, was the first infantry formation of which we have record. The supremacy of cavalry in the Middle Ages had been as much moral and social as technical. Developed because of its mobility, endowed with a total social and economic dominance, it had for centuries a virtual monopoly of military activity. Foot soldiers were simply despised auxiliaries. But the limitations on its effectiveness which had appeared in the thirteenth century when the house of Plantagenet tried to extend its rule into the mountains of Wales became yet more evident a hundred years later when the house of Austria tried to do the same in the mountains of Switzerland.

The original weapon of the Swiss mountaineers was not the pike which made them famous, but a simple axe, a halberd some eight foot long, with which they slaughtered the Austrian knights, hacking through their armour, not only when they trapped them in the defiles at Morgarten in 1315, but in the open field at Laupen in 1339 and Sempach in 1386; which bears out the view that the revival of infantry was due far more to moral, and thus social, factors than to any technical changes. The pike came a little later, in time for the Swiss victories over the Burgundian chivalry in 1476 and 1477. By then the Swiss pikemen had learned not only how to stand on the defensive like a huge and invulnerable hedgehog, but how to move as well, their phalanxes—'battles' several thousand strong—trundling forward and annihilating anything unwise enough to remain in their path. Moreover once they had assured the independence of their own cantons they were prepared to rent out their 'battles' to neighbouring armies; a natural enough way of supporting a population becoming too great for its own sparse pastoral economy.

But there was nothing in the Swiss tactics that could not be copied by others. Their neighbours in south Germany and Austria, equally impoverished, no less bellicose, began to raise their own formations, known as *landsknechts* or *lansequenets*. Their only difference from the Swiss was that they were drawn from a broader social spectrum: the nobility did not scruple, not only to raise and organize them, but to serve on foot in their ranks. Thereafter 'to trail a pike' became a perfectly acceptable form of military activity for the nobly-born in Germany, as later in England. As for Spain, heavy cavalry had never been a major component of the Christian armies in a country lacking forage and in the slow campaigns of the *reconquista*; and the Spanish kings found no problem in recruiting the poor, proud Castilian nobility to serve on foot in their wars.

So by the end of the fifteenth century 'battles', or 'battalions', of pikemen were a necessary part of every serious armed force; and increasingly there were being attached to them contingents of men armed with hand guns, especially the 'hooked' gun, *Hackenbüsche* or arquebus, which with its successor the musket was to be the infantry's firearm for another two hundred years. Infantry had arrived.

So, as we have seen, had artillery, cumbrous great pieces though they were, needing up to forty horses each to draw them. And paradoxically infantry and artillery restored a place on the battlefield to the horse. The infantry whose arrows or tenacity had, from Creçy onwards, made the mounted charge impossible could now be broken up by other infantry or by artillery fire. The charge, properly timed, might still be possible, and even if it was not, cavalry with firearms could now provide mobile fire power. But *cavalry*, be it noted; not the old chivalry of the feudal host, in which every man charged for himself, concerned as much with personal honour as with victory; but an arm to be combined with other arms, to be disposed of, like other arms, at the will of a commanding general.

The transition was to be slow. The French *gens d'armes* who took part in the Italian Wars between 1494 and 1529 certainly saw themselves in the same light as the *chevaliers* in the tales of Amadis de Gaul and Ariosto which were their fashionable reading. They tried to revive such anachronisms as single combat, and apparelled themselves more for conspicuous display than for the grim business of war about whose mundane and murderous nature infantry and gunners now had no illusions whatever. But elegant anachronism was to remain a characteristic of European cavalry for many centuries yet. Even in our day it has not totally disappeared.

But if the French *gens d'armes* who invaded Italy in 1494 were feudal in their ideology, there was nothing feudal about their economic base. Like the infantry and the gunners they now served purely for pay.

There had, as we have seen, been some stipendiary element in military service throughout the Middle Ages. For prolonged and distant campaigns tenants-in-chief and their followers needed more remuneration than the simple subsistence provided by their lord. The transition from receiving expenses for services rendered to fulfil feudal obligation, to rendering services for pay alone, was not a difficult one to make; especially for a class of men who had nothing to occupy their time except fighting and to occupy their minds except thinking about fighting. Since the twelfth century Europe had been no longer under siege. Its population and wealth was beginning to increase. The safety valve of the crusades was closing fast and, most important of all, the number of available fiefs had drastically shrunk. Where property could be indefinitely sub-divided, as in Germany, it ceased to provide economic support. Where primogeniture applied, as in England, younger brothers were left with little alternative except to seek their fortunes on a crusade or to turn mercenary. So the later Middle Ages saw the development of a larger military class than either the countryside or the available wars could support; and if no wars were available, not surprisingly the military class tended to manufacture its own.

The existence of these men, 'freelances' prepared to put their swords at the disposal of the highest bidder, at first enhanced the power of the princes—so long as they had money to pay for them. By the beginning of the fourteenth century, as we have seen, the kings of England and France had virtually placed their entire military force on a stipendiary basis. Even the greatest of their vassals provided an agreed number of troops by 'indenture', or contract. And once one prince was able to maintain a force in the field throughout a whole campaigning season or even a succession of campaigns, his competitors had to do the same. The money might, as we have seen, come from 'scutage', payment in lieu of military service from vassals whose services were not required, or from taxes or grants from the Church. But for the most part it had to come from the proceeds of trade: either from dues over which the prince had complete control, or from loans advanced by merchants, or from specific grants—usually in return for services rendered or privileges granted—made by representative bodies of the towns and other economically productive classes. Parliaments, Estates, assemblies representative of the non-military, non-noble sections of the community, began to figure largely in the capacity of the prince to make war.

But sooner or later the money ran out or the war came to an end, and the soldiers (as one can now accurately call them) were left without employment. They had no estates to go back to; often indeed they had no homes to go back to: their 'company' ('con pane', an organization providing them with subsistence as well as employment) was their only home.

In Italy, where allegiances were hopelessly disrupted by the Wars of Investiture which spanned a multiplicity of small wars, and where cash was always readily available, these mercenary bands were active and independent by the thirteenth century; sometimes providing straightforward military services to anyone willing to pay them, sometimes levying simple blackmail, of which more will be said in Chapter II. In France their activities reached an appalling peak a hundred years later. The Hundred Years War produced the greatest concentration yet seen of these mercenary companies on both sides, both of noble and of base-born soldiers of fortune, and in the intervals of fighting they simply lived off the countryside. From the middle of the fourteenth century until the middle of the 15th, these *écorcheurs*, as they were called with horrible descriptiveness, roamed France at will, collectively or individually pillaging, raping, and burning. They suspended their activities only during the increasingly brief and irregular periods when they were re-recruited into the service of an authority in a position to provide regular pay. Desperate French kings mounted campaigns in Spain and Hungary simply to get them out of the way. The situation began to improve only at the end of the Hundred Years War when the Crown was able to exploit the despair of the French merchants and obtained the right to levy a special tallage, the *taille des gens de guerre*, to put the royal forces on a regular basis. By the end of the fifteenth century the *taille* had become a permanent tax for which the authority of the Estates was no longer required. Thus royal finances were placed on a regular basis.

The original grant was made by the Estates to Charles VII of France in 1439. In 1444 he issued *ordonnances* whereby a number of the mercenary bands pullulating about the country were taken into the royal service on a permanent basis and used to forcibly disband the rest. There was no question here either of feudal obligation or of contractual 'indenture', with each captain finding and paying his own men in return for a lump sum. All officers were appointed by the Crown (and were thus truly *officiers*, office-holders); all, both officers and men, were directly paid by the Crown; and they resided in certain towns designated by the Crown. They were a fully stipendiary force, though not yet a national one: Germans, Scots, Italians were all part of this comradeship in arms. And they were formidable enough for the French king's wealthy rival Duke Charles the Bold of Burgundy to feel it necessary to imitate them twenty-five years later, raising an army which he at once squandered on the series of military adventures which brought him to grief at the hands of the Swiss and the French and prevented Burgundy from establishing itself, as it quite easily might have done, as one of the great nations of Europe.

The French kings were more prudent. For half a century they consolidated their territories by wise marriage, increased their wealth, and harboured their military strength. And when eventually Charles VIII set out for Italy in 1494 in quest of glory, adventure, power, and *virtu*, all those alluring prizes of the Renaissance, he did so with the finest army Europe had yet seen: Swiss pikemen making up the core of the infantry, a proud and noble cavalry, a train of bronze artillery which was to lay every castle it attacked in ruins, all drawing wages from a well-stocked treasury. It was an army not fundamentally different in composition from that which Napoleon was to lead to the same battlefields three hundred years later. Although the *gens d'armes* themselves would have indignantly denied it, the wars of the knights were over.

2

The Wars of the Mercenaries

With hindsight we can describe Charles VIII's force as the first 'modern' army, in that it consisted of the three arms deployed in various mutually supporting tactical combinations, and was very largely made up of men paid from a central treasury. Historians indeed normally date the beginnings of 'Modern European History' from the Italian Wars which opened with the French invasion of 1494. But few men at the end of the fifteenth century were conscious of a new era dawning, of any 'change of gear', in warfare or in anything else. Rather, indeed, the opposite.

In the last chapter something was said about the self-conscious archaism of the later Middle Ages and especially of the French chivalry which constituted the backbone of the royal armies. It was an archaism which was to last until the middle of the sixteenth-century; at least until the disappearance of that pair of princely rivals who embodied that feeling in their own persons and round whose quarrels all the politics of Europe became polarized, Francis I of France and the Emperor Charles V. The wars which filled the first half of the sixteenth century and were ended only by the stalemate at Cateau Cambrésis in 1559, were all entirely 'medieval' in their motivation; that is, they were fought to assert or to defend personal rights of property and succession, to reduce unruly vassals to obedience, to defend Christendom against the Turk, or the Church against heresy. Charles VIII invaded Italy to support the claims of the House of Anjou to the throne of Naples against those of the House of Aragon, and thence to lead a crusade to recapture Jerusalem. His successor Louis XII of Orleans prolonged the war to vindicate the claim of his house to the Duchy of Milan against the Sforzas and their Imperial patrons. The Emperor Charles V, after his election in 1517, inherited both these quarrels, the first from one grandfather Ferdinand of Aragon, the second from the other, the Emperor Maximilian; together with a third quarrel from one grandmother, Isabella of Castile, over the crown of Navarre, and a fourth from the other, Mary of Burgundy, over the lands which her father Charles the Bold had lost to the king of France. In all these contests his antagonist was the King of France, Francis I, who was also his unsuccessful rival for the Imperial Crown and who, in addition to assisting the rebellious Protestant princes of Germany against Charles's attempts to assert his Imperial authority over them, maintained a tacit understanding with the Turks; against whose really menacing advances in the Mediterranean Charles tried in vain to concentrate his forces. Thus at least for the first half of the century warfare still consisted of personal quarrels between individual princes over rights of inheritance, and not in any sense conflicts between states, let alone nations, over what they perceived to be their interests. As late as 1536 Charles V saw nothing odd in challenging his rival to single combat, and the challenge was accepted. The Pope had to intervene and the quarrel was patched up at a sumptuously extravagant display of mutual friendship at Nice, with both princes pledging themselves, as Christian princes had repeatedly for four hundred years past, to sink their differences in a joint crusade.

Still, the very concentration of these quarrels was politically and militarily significant. Admittedly both Charles and Francis had inherited, largely because of the prudent dynastic marriages of their predecessors, accumulations of territorial power beyond their capacity—or that of their successors—to sustain. Charles was to divide the Habsburg inheritance into the two more manageable halves, of Spain and Austria, and on the death of Francis's son Henry II in 1559 France was to relapse into civil war for fifty years. But the work of concentration was not to be undone, and a small number of clearly *sovereign princes*, with powers and rights of a distinctive kind, emerged from the ruck of contesting counts and dukes as the foci of a new order of power—political, financial, and military. The edges of the class were very blurred indeed, especially in Germany, where the spectrum stretched from major potentates like the Dukes of Bavaria and Saxony to the lords of a few acres in Swabia or Franconia; but what became increasingly clear, in the century of fighting which followed the death of Charles V, was that the relationship of these princes to one another was no longer determined by feudal rivalries or obligations, but by the facts of economic and military power, and that such power was increasingly to accumulate in the hands of the stronger. Only in Germany did the princelings survive, because the Habsburgs were too busy fighting the French or the Turks to deal with them. Even the states of the Italian peninsula, already reduced by the beginning of the sixteenth century to a bare half dozen, had by the end of that century very largely disappeared into the Habsburg maw. Only Savoy, Venice, and the Papal States retained more than the semblance of sovereignty.

For by the sixteenth century the price of independence was becoming very high indeed. It was not only the spectacular artillery trains which had to be paid for but the no less expensive and necessary professional infantry. So had fortifications which, as we shall see, were becoming ever more elaborate. The prince who had the political power to raise taxes from his subjects, or the credit to raise loans from the new banking houses like the Fugger and the Welser, could put armies into the field which steam-rollered their lesser opponents into oblivion. Certainly all this was easier said than done: the wars of Charles V and Francis I proceeded by fits and starts, as did those of Philip II of Spain, being brought to frequent sudden halts by spectacular royal bankruptcies. It was not until the second half of the seventeenth century that European princes acquired sufficient control of their territorial resources to maintain standing armies on a continuing basis and to wage prolonged campaigns almost as a matter of course. Nevertheless by the end of the sixteenth century the men, as it were, had become separated from the boys: it was clear which princes were capable of waging war on their own account and which were not.

This change was reflected in writings about war. Medieval writers from Aquinas onwards had always insisted that war could only be justly waged by a sovereign prince, a doctrine which was transcribed into that fourteenth-century vade mecum for gentlemen at arms, Honoré Bonet's *Tree of Battles*.[1] 'A man cannot' wrote Bonet 'take upon himself to do justice on another who has wronged him, but the prince must do justice between these men. But' he went on to confess a little ruefully, 'nowadays every man wishes to have the right of making war, even simple knights, and by law this cannot be'. The law in fact remained a dead letter so long as the prince commanded little more power than did his major vassals, and minor barons in impregnable castles could exercise unchallenged sway over their own countryside. The consolidation of princely power put an end to what medieval jurists called 'private war', and writers in the sixteenth and seventeenth centuries drew a firm line between wars fought by 'perfect states' and those conducted by private enterprise, which lost their last feudal sanctions and degenerated into private duelling or brigandage.

The 'perfection' of states, the emergence of sovereign princes both independent of superior authority and capable of making their writs run throughout their own lands, led to the extension throughout Europe of political doctrines long held in Italy, where such a system of states had developed a century or so earlier. These, crystallized most trenchantly by Machiavelli, maintained that states alone could be judge of their own interests; that, in Machiavelli's words, 'war is just when it is necessary', and that no higher authority could judge of that necessity. *Salus principis suprema lex.* This view was gradually endorsed by all the leading European jurists—Bodin in France, Gentili in Italy, Victoria in Spain. Although, they agreed, there were just and unjust wars, sufficient and insufficient cause for hostilities, the prince ultimately was the only judge, and usually both sides believed themselves to be in the right.[2] But these views were to be reconciled with older concepts of Christian unity in the study by the great Dutch thinker Hugo Grotius, *De Jure Belli ac Pacis*. Published in 1625 in the middle of the eighty-year war between Spain and the United Provinces,

this accepted the existence of sovereign states but saw
them as bound together, not by allegiance to any common
superior, but by the requirements of social existence, a Law of
Nations derived from natural law none the less binding
because there was no court to enforce it. This alone determined what were sufficient and insufficient causes of war, and
what were permissible and what impermissible acts within
war itself. Grotius virtually created the framework of thinking
about international relations, about war and peace, within
which consciously or unconsciously we still function.

Grotius wrote out of his own experience of almost continuous
warfare in north-west Europe. By the beginning of the seventeenth century the cheveleresque glamour which had attended
war a hundred years earlier had completely disappeared. 'I
saw prevailing throughout the Christian world' Grotius wrote
in 1625 'a license in making war of which even barbarous
nations would have been ashamed; recourse was had to arms
for slight reasons, or for no reason; and when arms were once
taken up, all reverence for divine and human law was thrown
away; just as if men were thenceforth authorized to commit
all crimes without restraint'.[3] It is time to examine in rather
greater detail the nature of this warfare to which Grotius
hoped to set some bounds.

The main characteristic was that indicated by the title of
this chapter. Whatever the rationale of wars during this
period, whether disputes over inheritance or, as they became
during the latter part of the sixteenth century, conflicts of
religious belief, they were carried on by a largely international
class of contractors on a purely commercial basis. There was
nothing new about this; it was only the continuation of a
process which had been going on, as we saw in the last
chapter, throughout the later Middle Ages; but now it had
become systematic and complete. Even where feudal obligation to knight service survived, as it did in France in the *ban*
and *arrière ban* in the early years of the sixteenth century, the
noblesse had either lost their military inclinations or preferred
to turn them to commercial profit. Indeed it was in France, as
we have already seen, that there first developed the rudimentary pattern for what would in the next century become a

professional army. But the *gens d'armes* of the *compagnies d'ordonnance* established in the fifteenth century, and the corresponding infantry 'legions' raised by Francis I and paid from the royal exchequer in the sixteenth, were only a small part of armies which, in France as elsewhere in Europe, were raised, maintained, and led into battle by a class of entrepreneurs whose only bond of loyalty to their employer was the assurance of cash payment, punctually and in full.

Military contractors of this kind had been flourishing in the Italian peninsula a couple of centuries before they took root north of the Alps. In Italy, as was mentioned in the last chapter, the fragmentation of the feudal structure by the Wars of Investiture left the nobility to their own devices, and the precocious development of an urban economy produced clients in the form of wealthy city-states who were prepared to pay them well for the hire of their military skills. In addition bands of foreign knights brought south by the German Emperors or washed up by the receding tides of the crusades were prepared, in the fourteenth century, to put their swords at the service of anyone who would pay them and to make life hell for anyone who did not. Among the most outrageous of these was the 'Great Company', a band nearly ten thousand strong and totally international in membership which persisted for fifteen years between 1338 and 1354 and ran what would now be called a protection racket on a very large scale. This group was succeeded a few years later by a mass of *routiers*, left unemployed by the ending of the Hundred Years War between France and England in 1361, who rode south from France under the standard of the Englishman Sir John Hawkwood and formed the famous White Company. Barbarous as these foreigners were, the Italians sometimes found that as employees they had advantages over their own warriors who were liable, not simply to cheat their employers, but to take over political power. But by the end of the fourteenth century the foreigners had become absorbed into the local aristocracy, or had gone home, or were dead, and the '*condottiere*' had become institutionalized.

'*Condottiere*' means simply 'contractors', being so called after the *condotta* which was their contract of service specifying the size of the force to be provided, the length of time it was to serve, and the scale on which it was to be paid. They came in all shapes and sizes, from the leaders of small bands to great nobles like the Gonzagas, the Este, or the Colonnas, who took their rewards in lands or fiefs. Some established themselves, as did Frederick of Montefeltro at Urbino, as independent princes with whom any contract was virtually a treaty between sovereign powers. Others either became politically dominant in the states which employed them, as did the Visconti and the Sforzas in Milan, or became their permanent professional advisers on defence and the commanders and trainers of the citizen levies.

The forces provided by the *condottiere* were predominantly mounted; that is, they consisted of 'lances' of at least one armoured man-at-arms with his train of attendant squire, page, and foot soldiers armed with spear or cross-bow, or, by the end of the fifteenth century, arquebus. The conduct of battle, especially in the hands of experts like Andrea Braccio and Francesco Sforza, became a subtle affair of feints and surprises, of forces held in reserve until the decisive moment, of manoeuvre as well as shock. Tactics and strategy became something of an art form. But their employers, having paid good money, demanded decisive results of a kind that the *condottiere* were often reluctant to provide. Machiavelli's scornful accusation that they fought bloodless battles is not borne out by the facts, but they certainly had the caution of all professionals, especially of professionals with a heavy personal investment in their own work-force which might be squandered by a single rash decision and which would be ruinously expensive to replace. Certainly their sophistication and indecisiveness made a poor showing when at the end of the fifteenth century Swiss pike battalions, French *gens d'armes*, and Spanish *tercios* converged on the peninsula, bringing a new thoroughness and with it a new bloodiness to the battlefields of Italy.

But this new phase was shortlived. Between the battles of Fornovo in 1494 and of Pavia in 1525 there were a dozen or so decisive engagements, but for nearly a hundred years thereafter the major battle almost disappeared from western

Europe. One can identify several reasons for this, including
the development of fortification and of fire power, which will
be considered later; but not the least important was the extension north of the Alps of military entrepreneurship on the
Italian model and with it the natural desire to conserve expensive plant. Cautious professional competence took the place of
the quest for glory in the planning and conduct of campaigns;
the caution of men who intended to see their investment in
armed forces pay off in terms of wealth, political influence, or
land. Professional competence did indeed demand courage,
endurance, on occasion self-sacrifice; there was no market for
cowards or blunderers in the business of war. But professional
soldiers do not get themselves or those they command killed if
there is some other way to gain their object; and not the least
effective way of terminating a campaign successfully was to
prolong it, avoiding battle and living off the enemy's country
until his money ran out, his own mercenaries deserted and he
had to patch up the best peace he could. The desertion by the
Swiss of the king of France before the battle of Pavia in 1525,
the inability of the Protestant German princes to put a strong
enough army in the field to defeat Charles V at Mühlberg in
1547, were only the most salient illustrations of the favourite
Latin tag of the period: *pecunia nervus belli*.

The most notorious and for a time the most sought-after
mercenaries in Europe were the Swiss, who having established
the independence of their cantons in the fourteenth century
with halberds and pike were driven, as we have seen, by the
sparseness of their economy to put their military skills at the
disposal of whoever was prepared to pay them—though increasingly, as the sixteenth century went on, this tended to be
the French. But the Swiss were very much in a class by themselves. In the first place war was for them a nationalized
industry. The negotiation of all contracts was in the hands of
the canton authorities, as was the selection of the troops,
among whom there reigned, during the campaign, the kind of
cantankerous democracy one finds in a successful trades union.
Secondly the Swiss were highly specialized. They produced
their great pike phalanxes, including men armed with swords
and halberds for close-quarter fighting, and that was all. They

did later accompany these with a few arquebuses and guns to protect their flanks, but basically they showed no inclination to diversify their techniques. Thus as shot became increasingly important and formations increasingly flexible the Swiss pike phalanxes became left behind like dinosaurs unable to adapt to a new environment, as much of a curiosity in the history of infantry as the English bowman of the later Middle Ages. Infantry fighting in the sixteenth century was to be shaped by professionals from Germany, and from Spain.

The great rivals of the Swiss, the south German *landsknechts*, adapted themselves more easily to the changing requirements of war, if only because for their leaders war and its associated techniques was a pure business proposition and not, as it tended to become with the Swiss, an inflexible social institution. The *landsknechts* made their reputation with the pike, but as 'shot' became more important on the battlefield, they recruited that as well. Their area of recruitment, both socially and geographically, was wider than that of the Swiss. The original *landsknechts* were drawn from the minor nobility of south Germany and their retainers. Early in the sixteenth century some of these knights began to expand and diversify their activities, recruiting cavalry 'lances' and artillery as well as pike and shot; and though German nobility remained for so long the backbone of these forces, minor knights who, without land or revenue, could not compete with the increasing wealth and display of their more fortunate neighbours, experienced troops of all classes and all nations were gradually drawn to their colours. By the end of the sixteenth century war was an international trade, and the proportion of nobility in these armies declined as the forces grew in size and attracted the adventurous or the desperate from every class. As the soldier had to provide his own arms and equipment the utterly indigent were excluded; but once enrolled, the prospects before a tough, ambitious, and unscrupulous young man of moving upwards in the social ladder were very fair. Pay was erratic; but if he survived diseases and battle, was not robbed by his colleagues, and did not drink or gamble his fortune away, then loot, ransom, and booty might provide him with the capital needed to set up business on his own account.

This anyhow was the prospect which lured men into becoming soldiers—a trade which by the end of the sixteenth century was classless, international, and precarious. The mercenary served any master: Protestant Germans happily fought under Spanish or French colours; Italian specialists served the queen of England or the Dutch; served them, that is, so long as they were paid. If they were not, they levied their subsistence and anything else they could get from the peasants and merchants among whom they were billeted. The Spanish Fury of 1574, when unpaid Spanish troops sacked and ransacked Antwerp, was only the most gruesome and spectacular example of the fate which befell countless towns and villages in north and central Europe in the late sixteenth and seventeenth centuries as armies grew larger and more unmanageable, their pay more irregular, and they crawled with their crowds of camp followers over the face of the land like locusts, destroying any community luckless enough to find itself in their path.

Not many of these soldiers of fortune attained great wealth and power. As so often happens, those did best who went in at the top. The men who set their stamp on the armies of the early seventeenth century were noble in their own right: the Marquis of Spinola, the Genoese who managed the military affairs of the king of Spain in the Netherlands; Count Ernest of Mansfield who raised an army for the luckless Elector Palatine in 1618 and then put his sword at the disposal of the highest bidder; the Bohemian Count Albert of Wallenstein who became not only the greatest military entrepreneur but the wealthiest man in Europe, controlling territories from the Baltic to Bohemia, his industries and estates producing armaments and supplies for the Imperial Armies on an unprecedented scale; Prince Bernard of Saxe Weimar, who raised forces first for Sweden, then for France. Bernard is particularly significant. He was to become the archetype of the minor German princes whose wealth and political influence rested on their capacity to provide a small, efficient army to whichever of their more powerful neighbours was prepared to pay for it; an activity to be most successfully pursued a little later in the century by the Electors of Brandenburg and their successors the kings of Prussia.

But the most interesting point about these great military entrepreneurs was that none of them succeeded in transforming their military effectiveness into political power. Wallenstein came nearest to it, with the huge estates he acquired in Mecklenburg. Had he lived he might have founded a new, legitimate dynasty whose territories would in time have become a sovereign state. But the wars were too continuous and too indecisive for these actors on the international stage to establish themselves as permanent forces, and the peace settlement in 1648, perhaps rather surprisingly, confirmed as *de jure* sovereign powers only those that had existed *de facto* when the fighting had begun in Germany thirty years before.

What of the armies which these men led? In essence they were not very different from that which we have seen Charles VIII leading into Italy in 1494: cavalry, infantry armed partly with pike, partly with hand guns, and artillery trains. Still, during this period such extensive developments took place within each of the three arms that by 1648 the armies fighting in Europe had more in common with those of Marlborough and Frederick the Great in the eighteenth century than with those of Francis I and Charles V in the sixteenth. These developments were due, not to any striking technological or scientific advances, but rather to a process of trial and error and to minor adjustments in the craft of weapon-making within a very stable and limited technological framework—a framework which was to remain fundamentally unaltered until the industrial transformations of the nineteenth century.

The most striking innovation of the late Middle Ages, firearms, were slow to take effect on the battlefield, and this was particularly true of artillery. In siege warfare the great guns were indeed to have profound and lasting effects, but as auxiliaries to the armies of the day their effectiveness was slight compared with their heavy cost. This made itself felt not only through the cost of the weapons themselves but in all the problems involved in deploying them on the battlefield. The eighteen guns proudly deployed by the Duke of Milan in 1472 required 522 pairs of oxen and 227 carts to draw them and their train. The French replaced oxen by horses and stone cannon-balls by the more destructive iron, but the whole

apparatus remained ineffably ponderous. By the end of the
sixteenth century it was generally reckoned that a single gun
needed a team of twenty to thirty horses to draw it, with a
further forty to pull its ammunition carts. The effect of these
lumbering convoys on the movement of armies over the un-
surfaced roads of Europe may be well imagined. War in the
winter was out of the question.

Nor when they reached the battlefield did the guns really
earn their keep. Their immobility meant that for maximum
effectiveness they had to be drawn up in front of the army, or
in the interstices of its formations, to give a single thunderous
salvo or 'greeting' to the opposing force. This might indeed be
horribly effective on the great squares of infantry, several
thousands strong, which were deployed in front of them, and
the immediate objective of the Swiss was always to overrun the
enemy guns before they could do any serious harm. But with
their slow rate of fire and the inaccuracy which resulted from
a combination of the recoil and of the 'windage' which gun-
founders prudently allowed between the projectile and the
barrel, they often did no harm at all. As Machiavelli put it,
'Great Guns do without comparison oftener miss the Infantry
than hit them, because the Foot are so low, and the Artillery
so hard to be pointed, that if they be placed never so little too
high, they shoot over; and never so little too low, they graze
and never come near them.' An English writer a hundred
years later, in 1604, said the same: 'Great artillery very seldom
or never hurt', so long as the infantry 'upon their giving fire
do but abase themselves on their knee till the volew be
passed.'[4] Gustavus Adolphus of Sweden was to change all that,
as much else, but throughout the sixteenth century the infantry
were to remain indisputably the queen of the battlefield.

Small arms were quicker to make their mark. Hand guns
were cheaper to produce and easier to use than cross-bows,
and though they could not sustain a comparable rate of fire,
their killing power against armoured horsemen was not less.
Early in the sixteenth century the arquebus gave way to the
long, heavy musket. This suffered the disadvantage of needing
a fork to support it and a lengthy and cumbrous process for
loading and firing; but it fired a ball which could crash

through the heaviest armour at 300 yards, and so was invaluable against charging cavalry. The English clung on to their beloved long-bows until almost the end of the century, their defenders arguing that they were lighter and handier than the musket, and enjoyed a higher rate of fire. But to be effective they required a prolonged and intensive training which was ceasing to be available even in England; and against armoured cavalrymen all seasoned campaigners preferred to rely on the heavy shot of the musketeer.

Defence against cavalry however was not the original function of 'shot'. As with the cross-bowmen whom they replaced, the hand gun men had the task of disorganizing and harassing the enemy force before the main encounter took place, when they slipped into the protection of the squares of pikemen who did the real business of fighting. It was the pikemen who stood steady to receive cavalry charges, checking horses at the end of their pikes, hauling off the riders with the hooks of their halberds, and finishing them off with their great swords. It was the pike squares which moved on the offensive, marching forward to the tap of drum and hacking their way through all opposition. In all sixteenth-century armies, save one, it was the man trailing the puissant pike who was held in highest honour.

The exception was the Spanish army, and since the Spanish *tercios* were to dominate the battlefields of Europe throughout the sixteenth century and the first third of the seventeenth, the exception is an important one. Spanish infantry was unusual in several respects. In the first place it originally consisted of conscripts: by the ordinance of Valladolid in 1494 one man in twelve between the ages of twenty and forty-five was declared liable for paid service at home or abroad. This was on the model of comparable French attempts to complement their *gens d'armes* with a class of professional infantry, but whereas the French repeatedly failed, the Spaniards succeeded in creating a solid core of expert professionals whose standards remained intact even when, later in the century, their armies came to consist largely of volunteers. Their success was at least partly due to the absence from Spain of the heavy cavalry tradition which had dominated French armies since the days of Charlemagne. The barren countryside of Spain did not lend itself to the breeding of cavalry horses. Mounted warfare during the *reconquista* had consisted of *genitours* skirmishing on light ponies. The tradition of the Spanish nobility was not, like that of the French and Burgundians, exclusively *cheveleresque*. It was therefore quite usual for a young Spanish nobleman to enlist in the infantry and serve in the ranks, though he probably had a servant and a couple of mounts to transport him and his baggage on the march.

When the armies of Ferdinand of Aragon invaded Naples in 1495 to vindicate his hereditary claim to that kingdom, they were initially not equipped with the pikes and arquebuses of his northern rivals, but, like the infantry of the Italian states, with swords and bucklers. This won the approval of such devotees of classical models as Machiavelli, but made no impression whatever on the Swiss pike squares. The Spanish commander Gonsalvo di Cordova quickly accommodated himself to the new style. He provided not merely pike but arquebuses in greater numbers than his adversaries; and like Edward III of England with his long-bows at Creçy, he transformed the arquebus from an auxiliary harassing weapon for the attack into a decisive one in the defence. This he did by using it in combination with field fortifications. The battle of Cerignola in 1503 set a pattern to be frequently repeated. The Spaniards allowed their enemies, both French cavalry and Swiss pike, to batter in vain against their fortified positions while the arquebuses picked them off, till they were too weakened to stand up to the Spanish counter-attack. The most triumphant example of all was to be Charles V's crowning victory at Pavia in 1525, when Francis I was himself taken prisoner. In the twenty-one years of fighting between the battle of Fornovo in 1494 and Pavia in 1525 we can see fire power moving from a purely auxiliary rôle to one where it was central and decisive; when the arquebus was no longer a minor appurtenance of the pike square, but when the pike square's principal function was to protect the shot. This the Spaniards recognized when they reorganized their infantry in 1534 into *tercios* of 3000 men each. Instead of having one musketeer to every six pikemen, as had been habitual in the Italian wars, they had equal numbers of each, and the musketeers received specialist pay. The process was beginning which was to end with the pike surviving only as a bayonet on the end of the infantryman's musket.

So the balance which at the end of the fifteenth century seemed to have tilted strongly in favour of the offensive, with the mobile pike phalanx, the great guns to blast away opposition, and the revival of cavalry shock action, had within twenty-five years been sharply reversed by the development of fire power on the battlefield. As always happens during such periods, the mobile arm entered the doldrums. Charging cavalry now found itself checked by a hedge of pikes or by trenches and barricades, and were picked off by musketeers. So they transformed themselves from an instrument of shock into one of mobile fire power. At first cavalrymen carried arquebusiers as pillion passengers. Then the development of the wheel-lock made it possible to ride with a firearm already loaded, and the cavalry for a time discarded the *arme blanche* in favour of the pistol—a weapon effective only if it was fired at five paces range or less. To enable these weapons to be effectively brought into play the cavalry devised the *caracole*, whereby successive ranks rode up to the enemy line, fired at point-blank range, and wheeled off to left and right. There is little evidence that this manoeuvre ever had very much effect.

All this provides additional explanation for the phenomenon which we have already discussed—the virtual disappearance of major battles from European warfare during the century which separated the battle of Mühlberg in 1534 from that at Breitenfeld in 1631. Only the indecisive battle of Niewport in the Netherlands in 1600, and the all too decisive battle of the White Mountain in 1621 when Bohemia was eliminated as an independent actor on the European stage, stand out as major exceptions. What we do see, and will continue to see for another century or so, is a long succession of sieges, with battle, when it occurred at all, as subsidiary to the major business of investing and relieving fortresses.

There was nothing novel about this. The castle had dominated medieval warfare, when the only resources available to the besieger were those of classical antiquity—catapults, battering-rams, escalade, and, most effective of all, hunger. The great gun brought this to an end: the demolition of the walls of Constantinople by Turkish artillery symbolized in this as in so many other respects the end of a long era in the history of western man. The high walls built to resist escalade, the even higher watch towers built to command the surrounding countryside, were pathetically vulnerable to the cannon balls crashing in to their base. Charles VIII had to besiege very few Italian fortresses in 1494; the mere reputation of his artillery brought them to terms.

But the answer was quickly found. Fire could only be countered by fire. At first the defenders improvised. They installed their own guns to fire through ports in the curtain walls, like cannon in a man-of-war, to keep the attack at a distance. They built and manned earthworks within any breaches made by the artillery of the besiegers. Then they began to abandon the vulnerable advantage of visibility for the more practical one of defence in depth: 'Our first care', as Machiavelli wrote, 'is to make our walls crooked and retort, with several vaults and places of receipt, that if the Enemy attempts to approach, he may be opposed and repulsed as well in the flank as in the front.'[5] This led to 'the bastioned trace', the arrangement of mutually supporting bastions projecting from the walls, so disposed as to give fire from the flank and rear against any assault on the walls or one another. The walls themselves were lowered to present the smallest possible target to enemy fire, and internally reinforced with earthworks. A moat would surround the fortress, itself covered by fire and perhaps protected by further outworks; and beyond it lay a smooth bare glacis, over which any assault was exposed to concentrated fire from all the defences.

Fortifications of this kind, at first improvised _ad hoc_ by the Italian cities in the last decade of the fifteenth century, spread all over Europe during the next fifty years, a matter as much of civic prestige as of military necessity—especially if Italian experts like Sanmichele or Sangallo could be obtained to design them. Originating as local, civic defences, they began to develop into that system of continuous frontiers which Vauban was to establish in France and Coehorn in the Netherlands in the seventeenth century. The kings of France turned Metz into a giant fortress which, barring as it did the high road from Germany into the heart of their country, may be seen without exaggeration as the direct ancestor of the Maginot Line. The United Provinces created a barrier of waterways and fortifications behind which they held out against Spain for eighty years and which now constitutes a frontier as unquestioned as the English Channel. These fortresses could not be taken by assault; nor could they be simply by-passed by armies whose supply convoys would then lie at the mercy of their garrisons. They had either to be masked, which meant detaching a force and weakening the main body, or they had to be invested; a process which, even if it did not culminate in an assault, consumed a great deal of time—and for sixteenth-century armies time was money, and money meant, or failed to mean, troops.

By the end of the Italian Wars in 1529 the broad outlines of siegecraft had been established by such experts as Pedro Navarro and Prospero Colonna. To counter the fire of the defence the besieging force took to the spade. First they surrounded the fortress with a containing line of trenches just beyond range of the defending batteries. From this they drove forward trenches in zig-zag lines at angles broad enough to prevent their being enfiladed by the fire of the garrison, and established concealed batteries at intervals along these lines. Once the trenches reached the edge of the glacis, sappers would drive mines under the fortifications and fill them with explosive charges; which the defence would counter with mines of their own. At the climax the besieger would unmask his batteries, concentrating their fire at the point which he had selected for a breach, spring his mines and launch his assault. This climax might come only after weeks of sapping and skirmishing in the trenches. The experiences of Tristram Shandy's Uncle Toby in Flanders, even those of the armies on the Western Front in the Great War, would not have seemed unfamiliar to soldiers who fought in Italy in the sixteenth century or the Low Countries in the seventeenth. This type of trench warfare, tedious, dangerous, murderously unhealthy, was to be the staple fare of the European soldier for over two hundred years.

All this—the. spread of fortification, the ascendancy of the defensive on the battlefield, the expense of mercenary troops and the professional caution of their leaders—explains why, for over a hundred years, warfare in Europe was so prolonged and so indecisive; smouldering away like wet wood, inflicting continuous damage on the countryside like some chronic disease to which the patient had philosophically if miserably resigned himself, never acting as a catalyst establishing a new pattern of politic order. In the Thirty Years War warfare reached the nadir of brutality and pointlessness portrayed in the etchings of Callot and the black humour of Grimmelhausen's prose. In order to survive at all, mercenary forces had to batten on the civil population. In order to survive at all civilians in their turn, their homes burned and their families butchered, had to turn mercenary. A soldier, in this period, was well described as a man who had to die so as to have something to live on. His condition was no better than that of the peasants he tormented. Armies were in a continual state of deliquescence, melting away from death, wounds, sickness, straggling, and desertion, their movements governed not by strategic calculation but by the search for unplundered territory. It was a period in which warfare seemed to escape from rational control; to cease indeed to be 'war' in the sense of politically-motivated use of force by generally recognized authorities, and to degenerate instead into universal, anarchic, and self-perpetuating violence.

From this condition there was, in western Europe, one great exception—the armies of the United Provinces; and they were exceptional for the very simple reason that they were regularly supplied and paid. If one could pay one's troops throughout the year, instead of hiring and firing them as occasion demanded, one could discipline them, train them, drill them, turn them in short into *professionals*. But this required ample and continuous supplies of money. Money in the necessary quantities could come only from trade. So before war could become a matter for professional armies there had to be fought, all over the world, the no less ferocious conflicts of the Merchants.

3

The Wars of the Merchants

In the last chapter we indicated how and why in the Europe of the sixteenth century wealth and military capability went hand in hand: *pecunia nervus belli* or, as the French phrased it no less laconically, *pas d'argent, pas de Suisses*. But by the beginning of the seventeenth century princes were finding it increasingly difficult to raise the money to pay their Swiss and the polyglot mercenaries who succeeded them. Such complaisant bankers as the Fuggers, the Welsers, and the Hochstetters who had made possible the campaigns of Charles V and Francis I had been dragged by their defaulting royal debtors into spectacular bankruptcy.[1] Princes had not yet established the bureaucratic fiscal systems which enabled them to draw continuously on the wealth of their subjects. Nor indeed had their subjects yet accumulated wealth on the scale necessary to finance the prolonged and indecisive campaigns which had, as we have seen, succeeded the spectacular forays of the early sixteenth century. So the capacity to sustain war and so maintain political power in Europe became, during the seventeenth century, increasingly dependent on access to wealth either extracted from the extra-European world or created by the commerce ultimately derived from that wealth.

There was in fact a continual interaction between the expansion of European enterprise overseas and the internecine conflicts between the Europeans themselves. Expansion provided further resources for those conflicts and was to a considerable extent generated by them. But initially the expansion of Europe originated in that yet older and more fundamental confrontation between the forces of Christendom and those of the Moslem world in the Iberian peninsula which had lasted

throughout the later Middle Ages; and was actually still going
on when a new phase in that conflict opened in the fifteenth
century with the Ottoman Turks overrunning the last relics of
Byzantine Christendom in the eastern Mediterranean and
penetrated through the Balkans to the heart of Europe. In our
concentration on events in western Europe we must not forget
that the struggle between Islam and Christendom, those two
great warrior cultures, did not come to an end in eastern
Europe until the eighteenth century.

In the western Mediterranean it was as part of their wars
with the Moors that, early in the fifteenth century, the Portuguese established themselves in North Africa, and obtained
Papal Bulls which authorized them to attack and subdue
Saracens, pagans, and other unbelievers inimical to Christ, to
capture their goods and territory and reduce their peoples to
perpetual slavery. It was within the medieval framework of a
crusade that Henry the Navigator sent off his expeditions along
the coasts of Africa in search of souls, Saracens, slaves, gold (to
enable him to 'maintain the gentlemen of his household'), and
of that mysterious potential ally against the infidel, Prester
John—the legendary Christian king in Africa who might need
succour in his own fight against the heathen and who would,
or so it was hoped, provide help to his European co-religionists
once he learned of their existence.

As a continuation of the struggle of Christians against Moslems, the expansion of Spain was only a shade less direct than
that of Portugal. The struggles on the Iberian peninsula had
fashioned the warrior-caste of Castile. For the Castilian knight
war was a way of life; so also, as the *reconquista* of the thirteenth
and fourteenth centuries pressed the Moslems in Spain ever
further to the south, was conquest and settlement. But by the
end of the fifteenth century Granada, that last elegant outpost
of Moorish civilization in Europe, had been overrun and the
whole of Spain had after seven hundred years been recon-
quered for Christendom. Almost at the same moment, the
discoveries of Christopher Columbus and his successors were
revealing new worlds beyond the seas to be conquered by the
Castilian sword and converted by the Christian cross. Five
centuries of religious war could not easily be bred out of the

Castilian nobility. Profit, adventure, glory, salvation, above all, *land*—all these now beckoned the *conquistadores* to extend their range beyond the seas. And once they arrived in the New World they conquered it, less because of any superiority in weapons over the indigenous populations, than because of their arrogant self-confidence, their horseborne-mobility, their toughness, and their fanaticism. They were the last of the warrior nomads who had broken into western Europe a thousand years before; nomads who had now taken the Cross and learned to sail.

Finally there were the more mundane rivalries in the Mediterranean between, on the one hand, the merchants of the Levant and of Italy, who comfortably monopolized the lucrative trades in silks and spices with the East, and those of the western Mediterranean, who were alert for any opportunity to break that monopoly. The Portuguese expeditions along the shores of Africa, originally commissioned by Henry the Navigator to extend the scope of Christendom, had by the 1480s the explicit objective of finding an alternative route to the East and tapping the trading system of the Indian Ocean; and this, in the last year of the fifteenth century, Vasco da Gama successfully did. That system, close knit and long established, was monopolized by Arabs and Indians who resented interlopers. It is unlikely that the Portuguese would have established and maintained themselves on the west coast of India, let alone (as they did with astonishing speed within the next two decades) in the Malayan peninsula and the spice islands of the Indonesian archipelago if they had not been equipped with those regrettably persuasive instruments, *ultima ratio mercatorum* as well as *regum*: guns.

The gun, as we have seen, was only one element in the development of land warfare during the Renaissance and by no means the most important. But in the development of naval warfare it was central. Until the fifteenth century war at sea was an extension of war at land. The object in battle was to close with the enemy vessel, board it, and overwhelm the crew. The most effective warship was thus, as it had been throughout antiquity, the oared galley, independent of wind or tide for its propulsion and carrying armed forces to board, fight, and

capture the enemy. Merchant vessels, needing capacious stow-
age, were dependent on sail, comparatively unmanoeuvrable,
and thus useless for fighting except against one another. It was
probably for defence against one another that they began to
equip themselves in the fourteenth century with the light guns
which were then becoming available; breech-loading affairs,
throwing a stone ball a couple of hundred yards, useful addi-
tions to the cross-bowmen but no more. Like the cross-bowmen
they were carried in high castles at each end of the ship so that
they could fire down on the decks of their enemies and if need
be on their own decks, if it ever came to boarding.

But then in the fifteenth century there came the Great Gun:
cast in bronze in a single piece, capable of bearing far higher
charges of explosive and firing heavier calibre of shot. A sixty-
pound iron ball fired upward of 300 yards could not only kill
men but bring down masts and rigging and smash through
decks. Mounted broadside and fired simultaneously they could
even sink ships. They were too heavy to mount in the castles,
but what need of castles if fire power prevented the adversary
from closing and boarding at all? So in the sixteenth century,
on sea as on land, fire power began to replace shock in battle.
In the seventeenth century, on sea as on land, it was to become
dominant. With guns mounted along flush decks, even merchantmen could more than hold their own against war galleys
whose guns could only be mounted in prow and stern. So for a
time the distinction between warship and merchantman almost
disappeared. It was to reappear in the eighteenth century
when gun power became all important and warships had to
crowd on board as many guns as the decks would hold if they
were to take their place in the battle line; but in the meantime
it was hardly worth putting a ship to sea unless it could both
carry a cargo *and* fight. It was a period when war, discovery,
and trade were almost interchangeable terms.

It was natural enough that vessels sailing into unknown
waters to discover and traffic with unknown peoples should go
armed, and equally natural that once the explorers had established trading posts they should protect them, whether against
European rivals or against unpredictable changes of mind on
the part of their customers, by establishing forts as well; even

where they had no intention of acquiring territory. The Portuguese empire in the East consisted simply of scattered trading posts. But it had to have its communications protected no less than did the Spanish Empire in the New World with its huge inland possessions; and the Portuguese needed this protection all the more once their European enemies began to extend hostilities to the high seas and beyond. For if war between Christian and infidel could be exported, so also could war between Christians; and if Spanish and Portuguese Catholics could be led to the East and to the New World by a mixture of religious enthusiasm and avarice, a search for souls and a search for gold, so also could their Protestant enemies when, in the second half of the sixteenth century, the dynastic conflicts of western Europe broadened into the Wars of Religion.

Sooner or later adventurers from north-west Europe would probably have broken in on the Iberian monopolies anyway. Much the same social forces were at work there as had driven the Castilian nobility to seek their fortunes beyond the sea. Internal pacification deprived the lesser nobility of their traditional occupations; inflation made it impossible for them to keep up traditional standards; laws of inheritance either divided estates into uneconomical parcels or reserved them for the eldest son, leaving the younger to seek their fortunes by their wits or their swords. In central Europe these were the men who became mercenaries. Those within reach of the coasts, the squireens of Normandy, Brittany, Devon, Cornwall, Holland, and Zeeland, provincials remote from the royal courts where they were anyhow far too poor to make their fortunes, turned to the sea. It was probably the same mixture of historical forces that inclined such men towards Protestantism; and the fact that they were so inclined made it an agreeable duty to turn 'privateer' and break in on monopolies established by authority of the Pope of Rome. The French Wars of Religion, the Revolt of the Low Countries, the memory of Marian persecutions in England provided incentive enough for Huguenot, Dutch, or English gentry to fit out vessels which might or might not be equipped with valid 'letters of marque' but were certainly equipped with guns, and set out either to smuggle

goods in and out of the Spanish Indies or quite simply to capture Spanish ships. Among west-country families in England,
as Dr Andrews so nicely put it, 'Protestantism, patriotism and
plunder became virtually synonymous';[2] and the same could
have been said of the lesser nobility of Zeeland and the *hober-
aux* round La Rochelle. Solid merchants, respectable courtiers,
the Queen of England herself were prepared to join in what
became, in the last third of the sixteenth century, an immensely
profitable bonanza. And when in 1580 the crown of Portugal
became united with that of Spain, the whole of the Portuguese
Empire from West Africa to the East Indies became fair game
as well.

Fair game, in the first instance, to the Dutch. For the United
Provinces, fighting an increasingly desperate battle for independence against the armies of Spain, the sprawling, badly defended Portuguese possessions provided a literally golden
opportunity. Capturing the trade of the Portuguese Empire
not only deprived the Spanish crown of a much-needed source
of wealth but furnished the Netherlands with funds for carrying
on their own war. Their early trading expeditions to the East
Indies in the 1590s paid dividends of up to 400 per cent. In
1602 they founded the East India Company which gradually
extruded the Portuguese from all but a handful of their trading
posts in the Indian Ocean and the East Indies. For the Dutch
merchant adventurers, indeed, the twelve-year truce with
Spain between 1609 and 1621 was an unwelcome interruption
to a course of unbroken predatory success. The moment it was
over a West India Company was formed to prey on the closed
trading system which the Portuguese had built up over the
past century in the South Atlantic: purchasing gold and ivory
from West Africa, transporting slaves under hideous conditions
from Africa to Brazil to work there on the sugar plantations,
exporting the sugar thus grown to Europe. This involved the
Dutch in an ill-judged and prolonged land war with the Portuguese in Brazil which swallowed many of their assets; but
none the less when in 1640 Portugal again separated itself
from the Spanish crown and sued for peace, both the East and
the West India Companies petitioned against it. The directors
of the former argued 'that the Honourable Company had

waxed great through fighting the Portuguese, and for this reason they had now secured a monopoly of most of the sea-borne trade in Asia; that they expected on average yearly return of between seven and ten millions; and that if they were allowed to continue in the same way, the above return would increase yearly.'[3] For the Dutch, as for other merchants of the period, war paid off handsomely.

We must not overestimate the contribution of these maritime enterprises to the growth of Dutch wealth in the seventeenth century. Only 0·2 per cent of the entire Dutch merchant fleet was involved even in the East India trade, and the West Indian venture was always suspect to the solid regents of Amsterdam.[4] The staple trade of the Dutch was still that with the Baltic, an activity so essential to their economy that they happily continued, throughout the Eighty Years War with Spain, to act as carriers for the naval stores which Spain needed to maintain the fleets which protected Spanish commerce against Dutch attacks. This enabled the Dutch to earn the cash with which to pay the forces to protect their frontiers against the Spanish armies. It was an arrangement which contemporaries and posterity have found equally puzzling, but it worked to everyone's satisfaction.

Still, Dutch overseas enterprise was undeniably lucrative: after 1634 the East India Company paid a regular dividend which fluctuated between 12½ and 50 per cent. It all contributed to that prosperity which made the United Provinces such a pleasant oasis in the wilderness to which Europe was reduced by the Thirty Years War; a prosperity which gave the Dutch security behind their river-lines and fortifications, which enabled them to pay, discipline, and professionalize their troops, and which made them the envy of new maritime predators who were gathering strength in their wake.

Like sensible merchants, the Dutch tended to go where the pickings were easy, so they did not break their teeth against the increasingly formidable fortresses which the Spaniards erected in the Philippines or the West Indies. For the Spaniards were not, like the Portuguese, traders. The conquistadors had gone to Mexico and Peru to settle, convert, and rule, and their possessions were too far inland to be disturbed by the incursions

of heretical maritime interlopers. But they had also come
in search of that very much more gentlemanly source of
wealth which had haunted the imagination of a specie-
starved medieval Europe—gold. And though they did not find
much of that, they did find silver in the hitherto unimaginable
quantities which was to help Spain dominate Europe for a
generation and to transform the Western economic system.

The fleets which ferried this treasure back to Europe tanta-
lized Spain's enemies for the best part of a hundred years; not
simply because of the tempting prize they offered in themselves but because to intercept them seemed the obvious way
of slicing the Spanish economic jugular vein. This was the
strategy so eloquently urged on Elizabeth by Hawkins and
Essex: 'The hurt that our State should seek to do him [the
King of Spain]' urged Essex, 'is to intercept his treasures,
whereby we shall cut his sinews and make war on him with
his money.'[5] But this was very much more easily said than
done. The Dutchman Piet Heyn did indeed have a well-
deserved stroke of luck when in 1628 he surprised and captured the entire *flota* at Mantanzas, thus ruining Spanish credit
in Europe and wrecking her Caribbean trading system for
years. But apart from that, against the assiduous professional
care which the Spaniards took to safeguard their treasure, the
sporadic, haphazard, ill-planned, and ill-fated attempts by a
whole succession of miscellaneous sea-dogs from Hawkins on-
ward proved in vain. The treasure fleet was to fall again only
thirty years later to the superior professional planning and the
organized naval power of Admiral Robert Blake in 1657.

The real profit in the West Indies lay in smuggling and
piracy. The privateers of the sixteenth century virtually institutionalized themselves in the Caribbean in the seventeenth,
trading and raiding indiscriminately under any flag that came
in handy. The first English and French settlements in the
Caribbean were simply bases from which their privateers
could operate. The Dutch provided them with naval equipment, technical advice, and a guaranteed market for their
goods. The English and the French also established themselves
further north in Canada, New England, and Newfoundland,
and their disputes in these bleak latitudes added further to the

European frictions of the early seventeenth century. But it was the Caribbean that remained the focus of attention for another hundred years as the English and French slowly turned their attention from smuggling to the cultivation, in cut-throat competition with one another and with the Dutch, of that new source of wealth: sugar.

The Dutch, once they had broken in to a rival system, were usually prepared to share the spoils with anyone, even their mortal enemies, so long as they could make a profit from it. The English and the French on the other hand were concerned to build closed, antagonistic, mutually exclusive trading systems, each of which could flourish, they considered, only on the ruins of the other. As the French Minister Jean-Baptiste Colbert wrote, with frank relish, to Louis XIV in 1670: '[Your Majesty] has undertaken a war of money against all the states of Europe. He has already conquered Spain, Italy, Germany, England and some others, in which he has caused great misery and want, and by despoiling them he has enriched himself. Only Holland is left . . .'[6] France, in his view, could rise to power and wealth only on the ruins of her rivals. It was a doctrine which became endemic throughout Europe by the latter half of the seventeenth century.

By the end of the Thirty Years War in 1648, therefore, the combination of religious zeal, quest for plunder, and desire for honest trading profit which had inspired European expansion and maritime rivalries for the past two hundred years was becoming systematized and simplified into a straightforward conflict of and for state power—a conflict fought out predominantly between the Dutch, the English, and the French. Trade was seen as desirable because it increased not simply the wealth of individual merchants but the power of the state— and that, devoted to the protection and promotion of trade, could create yet more wealth. 'What nation soever', wrote an Englishman at the time of the first Navigation Act in 1651, 'can attaine to and continue the greatest trade and number of shipping will get and keepe the Sovereignty of the Seas, and consequently the greatest Dominion of the World.'[7] And the nation which appeared to be getting the greatest trade and number of shipping, especially after the Peace of Westphalia in 1648 brought the Eighty Years War with Spain to a close and it could concentrate uninterruptedly on maritime activities, was the Dutch.

Between the Dutch and the English there seemed, to contemporaries, to be a direct and irrepressible conflict of interest. Quarrels over fisheries and protocol on the high seas were mere pretexts. The basic cause was expressed in words attributed to General Monck on being asked what reason should be given for declaring war on the Dutch: 'What matters this or that reason? What we want is more of the trade the Dutch now have.'[8] So in three wars, in the confined spaces of the North Sea, Dutch and English fleets clashed, on the whole inconclusively, and took their first steps in learning organized naval tactics and strategy: tactically, how to avoid bloody mêlées which led to no clear result and instead to keep station in line ahead and so maximize the effectiveness of their guns; strategically, the value of blockade as a way of bringing direct pressure on the enemy government and people.

The French were not far behind: 'Only Holland is left,' Colbert had said, in the memorandum we have already quoted,

and it fights with great reserves: its commerce with the North, which brings it so many advantages and such a great reputation for its sea forces and navigation; that of the East Indies, which bring it every year 12m in cash; its commerce with Cadiz and that with Guinea and an infinity of others in which its strength consists and resides . . . This war, which consists only in wit and energy, and of which the spoil of the most powerful republic in Europe must be the prize of victory, cannot soon be finished. Or, to put it better, it should be one of the chief objects of the application of Your Majesty during his whole life.

It is possible that Colbert deliberately overdid the military imagery, to catch the attention of a king who considered war to be 'la plus digne et la plus agréable occupation des souverains', but he only stated rather more sharply what was generally accepted among both statesmen and merchants in the latter part of the seventeenth century: that trade was a form of war. War, to paraphrase Clausewitz, was a continuation of commerce with an admixture of other means. Nowhere was this view to be held more strongly than in the England of the early eighteenth century, when she took the place of the Dutch as Europe's leading commercial power; and we find British merchants in 1745 viewing the prospect of peace with France and Spain with quite as much alarm as the Dutch had viewed the prospect of peace with Spain and Portugal a hundred years earlier. 'It is more in the true interest of these Kingdoms in general,' stated one of them, 'that we should continue in a state of war with them, so that war is carried on only by sea, than in a state of peace ... our commerce in general will flourish more under a vigorous and well-managed naval war, than under any peace which should allow an open intercourse with those two nations.' Another contemporary writer urged the government 'so to distress the commerce and navigation of our ever-restless enemy, as to disable them in future times from maintaining that lucrative competition with us in trade, they have too long done.'[9] If Colbert saw commerce as an instrument of state power, the merchants saw state power, especially naval power, as a necessary means of increasing their commerce.

The whole mercantilist argument had indeed an elegance and coherence in theory which was not, unlike so many elegant economic arguments, disproved in practice. Trade did engender wealth; wealth, if the government could get at it, could be translated into fleets and armies; fleets and armies, if properly equipped and commanded, did increase state power. As the English writer Charles Davenant observed at the end of the seventeenth century, 'Nowadays the whole art of war is reduced to money: and nowadays, that prince who can best find money to feed, cloath and pay his army, not he that has the most valiant troops, is surest of success and conquest.'[10] And during the quarter-century of wars between 1689 and 1713 when the British, the Dutch, and their continental allies engaged in almost continuous struggle against the France of Louis XIV—a struggle both for wealth and for power—it was the greater capacity of the maritime powers to mobilize their resources, particularly their financial resources, that eventually carried the day. To the Bank of England and the Treasury, the whole mechanism which came into being for the raising of loans and the establishment of credit, must go at least as much responsibility for ultimate British success in that war—as indeed in all subsequent wars—as is due to the generalship of Marlborough and to the professional competence of armed forces by land and sea. There was little point in winning—let alone risking—a major battle if there were not to be any resources left over for a campaign the following year.

The growing capacity of European governments to control, or at least to tap, the wealth of the community, and from it to create mechanisms—bureaucracies, fiscal systems, armed forces—which enabled them yet further to extend their control over the community, is one of the central developments in the historical era which, opening in the latter part of the seventeenth century, has continued to our own time. In the eighteenth century this process was to gather increasing momentum, but until then it was a very halting affair. Its progress can be traced as clearly as anywhere else in the gradual acquisition of state control over the means of making war— over that violent element in European society which, as we saw in the last chapter, had in the early seventeenth century virtually escaped from control and was feeding on itself, so that the historian has to speak not so much of 'war', or 'wars' as of (to borrow Sir George Clark's terminology) a *mêlée*.[11]

Such a term could have been applied quite as appropriately to war at sea as to war at land. In the sixteenth century the maintenance of a navy was an even more expensive business than the upkeep of an army. Armies could be, and were, hired or levied *ad hoc* and paid off at the end of a campaign. But even if sailors could be hired and fired as occasion demanded, ships had to be built and had to be maintained, war or no war. The capital investment was enormous. They required an infrastructure of dockyards, shipwrights, pilots, cartographers, ordnance experts—the nucleus in fact of a paid, permanent, professional service. It was hard enough for Samuel Pepys and Colbert to create such a force, and find the money to pay it, in the latter part of the seventeenth century. A hundred years earlier it had been virtually impossible. American silver did something to ease the task for Spain, but the effort bankrupted the Elizabethan government. When the Stuarts tried to restore the Royal Navy by reviving the tax of Ship Money, the result was constitutional catastrophe.

What could be done to assert naval power when there were no resources to pay for it? All European princes has recourse to the same expedient: the issue of 'letters of marque', authorization to private vessels to distress the enemies of their sovereign and take prizes, out of which the sovereign would take his or her share of the proceeds. The privateer was thus in a way the maritime equivalent of the *condottieri*. But between the privateer equipped with letters of marque authorizing him to distress the enemies of his sovereign, and the buccaneer equipped only with guns who distressed anyone he could catch, the line was very thin indeed. And the latter abounded. In 1595 a Spanish official in the West Indies complained that 'for the last four years . . . corsairs are as numerous and assiduous as though these were ports in their own countries. . . . Not a ship coming up from outside escapes them, nor does any which leaves the harbour get past them.'[12] But piracy was no less rife in the Indian Ocean, where large Dutch or Portuguese merchantmen with their priceless cargoes were frequently hijacked; and the North Sea and the Channel, where freebooters operated out of Dunkirk almost unhindered; while the pirates of the Barbary coast exercised a reign of terror not only in the Mediterranean but throughout the Atlantic, on occasion raiding the south coast of England in search of plunder and galley slaves. The early seventeenth century in fact 'saw the creation of great areas of savage, unorganised conflict through which only the very well-armed or the very inconspicuous could move with any confidence.'[13]

Very slowly this problem was solved as governments extended control over the bases from which the pirates operated. After 1650 British, Dutch, Spanish, and French officials in the West Indies sank their differences and made common cause against piracy, and by the end of the century they had almost eliminated it. But they could not control the shores of North Africa, from which corsairs continued to operate until the nineteenth century. So whether he went out looking for trouble or not, the European trader had learned to expect it, and went armed.

As an auxiliary arm of the state the privateer also survived into the nineteenth century, his value dwindling as naval vessels became swifter and more powerfully gunned, until with the advent of the ironclad man-of-war he virtually disappeared. But as a commerce raider he retained his value until the Napoleonic Wars, especially when he was supported and encouraged on the scale practised by France in the War of the Spanish Succession between 1701 and 1714.

In that 'guerre de course' the Colbertian principle of mobilizing private commercial resources as instruments of state policy was followed through with logic and efficiency, in pursuit of a strategy carefully thought out by that other great French strategic thinker, Sebastien le Prestre de Vauban. Privateers in France became organized as a state concern on the lines of a large trading company. Private capital provided the money, but the crown provided the ships, fitted them up in royal arsenals, recruited the sailors and subjected them to military discipline. These privateers worked closely with the royal French Navy. The men-of-war attacked British and Dutch convoys so as to force their vessels to scatter and become a prey to the privateers, while the latter operated on a scale intended to compel the enemy to adopt measures of trade defence so exorbitantly expensive as to make the continuation of the trade itself not worth his while. They operated mainly in the Channel and the North Sea; but 'they went as far as Spitzbergen to destroy the Dutch whale fishing, to the Azores to intercept the Portuguese trade from Brazil, to St Helena for Dutch and English cargoes from the Far East.'[14] The carefully planned and lavishly equipped expeditions of Jean Bart, de Forbin, and Duguay Trouin were a far cry from the sporadic enterprises of Drake and Hawkins a hundred years before.

But the greatest examples of state encouragement of private enterprise in order to increase its own wealth and power were the chartered companies, of which the English East India Company, founded in 1600, was the oldest and the longest lived. Its foundation was imitated two years later by the Dutch East India Company and, as we have seen above, in 1621 by the Dutch West India Company. The various English companies founded in the early seventeenth century to settle

North America, with their courts and their governors, were comparable in the plenary powers they enjoyed to negotiate with foreign potentates, to make war or peace, to establish garrisons, to purchase armaments, and to raise armies and fleets. The French followed suit more slowly but, once Colbert arrived on the scene, with passionate intensity. Whereas the Dutch and English companies were primarily associations for the promotion of private wealth from which the state would get, in one way or another, a substantial dividend, the French companies, obsessively supervised in every detail of their operations by Colbert himself, were quite explicitly instruments and agents of French power. The French East India Company was founded in 1664, with its entrepôt at Madagascar, to compete in the Indian Ocean. Their West India Company was established the same year, with its writ running from West Africa, through the Caribbean, north to Canada. The *Compagnie du Nord* was intended to chisel the Dutch out of the Baltic trade; the Levant Company, to control the Mediterranean. These companies Colbert described quite openly as armies, brought into being to wage that war specifically on the Dutch to which he urged Louis XIV to dedicate his life. And perhaps it was because they were so explicitly instruments of state power, because they were so obsessively controlled from the centre, that they failed to flourish anything like as successfully as did their Dutch and British rivals.

These chartered companies continued to operate beyond the seas as independent actors on the world scene, making war and peace as well as money, until the nineteenth century, when the opening up of the interior of Africa saw the creation of a further generation of chartered companies whose activities, under the direction of such equivocal figures as King Leopold II of the Belgians and Cecil Rhodes, prolonged the phenomenon almost until our own days; if one considers the activities of the *Union Minière* in Katanga, indeed, to well within our own days.

But by the eighteenth century the warlike activities of these concerns, like those of small-scale privateers, were increasingly subordinated to, and dependent on, state control. The navies of the European powers had become entirely professional, their ships built in royal dockyards, commanded by full-time regular officers, their types categorized and specialized, their activities co-ordinated and controlled in accordance with centrally-planned strategies. Certainly a vital element in those strategies was always the restriction of the trade of the enemy to the benefit of one's own: trade protection and blockade was always to occupy the bulk of the Royal Navy's time and attention. But one cannot for that reason class the great naval struggle between France and Britain which lasted with few interruptions from 1741 until 1815 as just another 'war of the merchants'. Nor did such men as Boscawen and Hawke, Rodney and Nelson think of themselves as mercenaries hiring their services to the state and getting a cut of the proceeds, even though 'prize money' remained a valued part of naval emoluments. They were, or saw themselves as, professional naval officers; and what they were, or thought they were fighting for, was something which they called their 'country': its prestige, its wealth, its greatness, its power. By the end of the eighteenth century *professionalism* and *patriotism* had become major elements in wars between the states of Europe.

4

The Wars of the Professionals

By the eighteenth century European wars were being conducted by professional armed forces of a kind with which we would be familiar today. Their officers were not primarily members of a warrior caste fighting from a concept of honour or of feudal obligation; nor were they contractors doing a job for anyone who would pay them. They were servants of the state who were guaranteed regular employment, regular wages, and career prospects and who dedicated themselves to the service of the state, or rather of their 'country' (to use a more emotive term) come peace, come war. It was only with the development of these full-time professionals that it became possible to draw any clear distinction between the 'military' and the 'civilian' elements in society.

Their evolution was gradual and uneven. Among the Prussian officer corps, feudal and even pre-feudal concepts of personal obligation to a 'War Lord' remained powerful until the twentieth century. The French officer-corps until the Revolution still consisted very largely of quarrelsome and self-indulgent *noblesse* with whom the state bureaucracy had to conduct a running fight. The development of the British Army from a collection of independent and heterogeneous regiments to a centralized and unified force is even today still far from complete. Yet by 1700, the essential outlines were there: a state machine responsible for, and capable of, maintaining a full-time force on foot in war and peace—paying, feeding, arming, and clothing it; and a coherent hierarchy of men with a distinct sub-culture of their own, set apart from the rest of the community not only by their function but by the habits, the dress, the outlook, the interpersonal relations, the

privileges, and the responsibilities which that function demanded.

The development of state power and organization made such
professional forces possible; but the development of military
practice and technology made them, functionally, almost
essential. In noting this interaction one cannot ignore another
which developed simultaneously: the manner in which the
development of professional armed forces, itself made possible
by the increasing control acquired by the state over the
resources of the community, enabled the state to acquire yet
greater control over those resources by serving as an instrument,
not only of external defence but of internal compulsion.[1] The
existence of armed forces capable of coercing reluctant Estates
into voting subsidies and reluctant taxpayers into paying taxes
to increase those armed forces was an alarming residuary
power at the disposal of the crown. It was enough to frighten
the architects of the British constitution in 1688 and their
imitators across the Atlantic a century later into circumscribing
most narrowly the power of the executive to maintain armed
forces in time of peace. Here one can refer only in passing to
the difference not only in the constitutional and political
system but in the entire cultural pattern between a country
like the United Kingdom, whose fortunate geographical position enabled her for centuries to regard an army as an optional
luxury, and Prussia, of which the German historian Hans
Delbrück could write 'The history of the development of the
army . . . is simultaneously the history of the Prussian State.'[2]

It was, as has been suggested in an earlier chapter, the
United Provinces which took the lead in the development of a
professional force. The wealth which the Dutch derived from
their overseas trade enabled them, almost alone among the
states of the early seventeenth century, to keep their forces
under arms throughout the year. And because they could pay
their soldiers regularly and well, they could make them do
two things which all other mercenaries in Europe regarded as
being beneath them. They could make them *dig*, and they
could make them *drill*; both activities of enormous importance
in increasing the power of the defensive.

The importance of the first is self-evident. It was the creation and maintenance of continuous lines of entrenchments, together with the natural defences provided by waterways and the permanent fortifications built by Coehorn, that made the United Provinces so impregnable for so long. The second activity, drill, was significant mainly in relation to the growing importance of fire power on the battlefield. It was Prince Maurice of Orange who, at the end of the sixteenth century, first saw clearly that fire power was now the decisive element rather than shock: that the pike was there to protect the musket, not the other way round. It was thus necessary to devise both *formations* which would maximize fire power, and *procedures* to ensure its continuous and controlled delivery. Instead of the pike squares several thousand strong with 'sleeves' of protective shot which had become normal in the sixteenth century, Maurice adopted elongated formations of musketeers some ten deep, with pike formations interposed simply to protect them against charging cavalry; the musketeers countermarching in their files, reloading as they did so, so that their front rank was always giving continuous fire.

This development in the conduct of battle demanded a greatly heightened degree of control on the battlefield itself: control of movement, control of fire, above all (now that the troops were no longer huddled together in great masses but strung vulnerably out in line) *self*-control. For this drill was needed, and, more than drill, *discipline*. The concept of discipline has become so much a part of our idea of military life that it is hard for us to realize what a new phenomenon it was in European warfare in the seventeenth century. Feudal men-at-arms were totally, gloriously undisciplined; so were the *landsknechts* and the *tercios*, men who simply arrived with their tools and did their job and who regarded one another very much as equals, distinguished by function but not by status. Discipline was not a welcome concept: in spite of their pay, the rate of desertion from the armies employed by the United Provinces was high. Nor was it an entirely original one. In the same way as Maurice, like so many other cultivated soldiers of his age, scanned the military textbooks of antiquity, especially the frequently reprinted works of Aelian and Vegetius, for ideas about the organization and deployment of armies derived from the Greeks and the Romans, so did his more scholarly associates (particularly Justus Lipsius of the University of Leyden) rediscover those Stoic philosophers whose teaching about self-control, self-abnegation, and submission to authority provided the necessary counterpart to the mechanism of Roman military models, the spirit of which alone would make them work. This stoical philosophy of self-sacrifice and obedience harmonized well with the sober life-style of Protestantism. It proved more acceptable, not only to the Dutch, but to the Swedes, the Scots, the Brandenburgers, and not least the troopers of the New Model Army in England, than it did to Spaniards, and French and Italians among whom individualism, sense of honour, love of *panache*, and quest for glory continued to play a very dominant rôle.

Although Maurice and his colleagues studied and discussed all these questions, practised the formations, drilled the troops, and actually founded a military academy at Siegen where Protestant *noblesse* could be educated in the new doctrines, the infrequency of pitched battles gave little chance to try them out in practice. But among Maurice's pupils was a Swedish nobleman, Jacob Delagardie, who became military instructor to the prince who, as Gustavus Adolphus, ascended the throne of Sweden in 1611 and was to spend the remaining twenty years of his life fighting, first his Baltic neighbours and then, when their tentacles began to extend northwards towards his own possessions, the encroaching armies of the Habsburgs. So Gustavus had greater opportunities to put into effect and develop the practices of the Dutch school; and he had a different kind of army to do it with.

Feudalism had more or less by-passed Sweden. Among their lakes and forests the Swedes had been able to retain, as an effective form of military organization, that general obligation to military service which the English and the Germans had been forced to abandon in the ninth century before the onslaught of the Norsemen and the Magyars. In the sixteenth century the Vasa dynasty had formalized this into systematic conscription to provide a force capable of sustaining their prolonged campaigns against the Danes and the Poles. So when Gustavus came to the throne he found to hand a national

army which to contemporary eyes must have looked remarkably archaic but to ours appears no less remarkably modern.
Gustavus turned it into an effective long-serving force. Service
lasted for twenty years, but only one man in ten was called on
to serve, and the rest were taxed to provide his equipment. So
in practice the Swedish army was a force composed of long-
serving regular troops. Local communities were made responsible for finding their quota of men, but exemptions from
service were granted—as under later conscription laws in
Europe—to only sons of widows, to men with brothers already
serving, to workers in mines and munitions industries, to the
nobility (who served as officers anyway), and the priesthood.
This army when at home did not receive any pay from the
royal treasury but lived, in an orderly and organized way, off
the land. When it went abroad it had to be paid, and things
became more difficult. Sweden was a poor country and pay
rapidly got into arrears. Gustavus in fact found it cheaper to
use his own troops for garrison duties at home and to rely on
local mercenaries to do most of the fighting. At the time of his
death in 1632, of the 140,000 men under his command, rather
less than one tenth were actually Swedes, and the rest were
provided either by local recruitment in Germany or by such
paid associates, part employees, part allies, as Bernard of
Saxe-Weimar. But all adopted and were trained in the Swedish
system of war, whose effectiveness was revealed when at the
battle of Breitenfeld in 1631 the Habsburg forces suffered a
cataclysmic defeat which transformed the pattern of power in
Europe.

Gustavus was to be killed the following year and his armies
were thereafter slowly to disintegrate. But he had provided a
pattern for the conduct of war to which the states of Europe
were to aspire with increasing success for the rest of the century.
His long-serving soldiers, both officers and men, were paid,
clothed, armed, and equipped by the crown and commanded
by the monarch himself or his immediate lieutenants. Discipline was severe and enforced by courts martial. Supply and
logistics were recognized as a state responsibility, even though
it was one that the Swedish state found too heavy to sustain far
beyond its own borders; so the Swedish armies were able, at

least initially, to move without the vast concourse of camp followers, many times their own size, which accompanied other forces in the Thirty Years War. On the battlefield they deployed in the flat formations practised by Maurice of Orange; but a lighter musket and constant practice made their rate of fire and reloading so rapid that the depth of infantry formations could be reduced from ten deep to six or even less; the musketeers even being able to deliver, on rare and awful occasions, a simultaneous salvo of fire.

Cavalry and artillery were transformed as well. Instead of practising the elegant but ineffective *caracole*, Swedish cavalry learned again how to use the *arme blanche*, how to charge with the sword in a disciplined mass, an instrument of shock more terrifying because more concentrated and more controlled even than the chivalry of the Middle Ages. It was to be a tactic which Oliver Cromwell's Ironsides were to bring to perfection in the English Civil Wars.

As for artillery, Gustavus worked incessantly to overcome its basic disadvantage: *immobility*. The answer was provided by the discovery that the range of cannon did not necessarily increase with the length of the barrel; that their length indeed could be halved, and their weight accordingly, without any decrease in their effectiveness. This discovery, and the many other improvements in gun-founding introduced by the great Swedish ironmaster Louis de Geer, a major industrialist who dominated the economic life of western Europe in the first half of the seventeenth century, made possible the introduction of mobile field artillery; guns which could be moved—if necessary manhandled—on the battlefield, which could fire either solid shot or case-shot against infantry as circumstances demanded and whose rate of fire, previously two or three rounds an hour, began to compare not unfavourably with that of the musketeers themselves.

Finally, perhaps the most important innovation of all, these three arms—two of them maximizing fire power, one offensive shock—were taught to co-operate and to manoeuvre on the battlefield; an operation of great difficulty which needed not only clear-sighted and quick-witted commanders but an integrated structure of hierarchical control and instantaneous, disciplined response. It was something seldom achieved; when Gustavus himself was not there, very rarely indeed. But for almost the first time since the far simpler and smaller conflicts of antiquity it was now possible for armies not simply at the outset of a battle but throughout its course, to be the instruments of a single controlling will. It was indeed thanks to all these developments during the first half of the seventeenth century that the second half witnessed the appearance of so many outstanding generals: Turenne and Luxemburg, Montecuccoli and Eugene of Savoy: and John Churchill Duke of Marlborough, the greatest of them all.

So Gustavus provided a blueprint, an indication—it would be unwise to put it any more strongly than that—of the way in which the inconclusive and generalized violence into which warfare had degenerated, and into which its tendency is always to degenerate, might be got under total control; how the violent element which permeated European society could be canalized and put to the purposive, legitimized uses of the developing state machine; how brigands could be turned into soldiers, anarchic violence into the intelligent and controlled use of force by authorities recognized according to accepted value-systems as legitimate. Until this was done, no orderly state-system in Europe was really possible; but it could not be done until the mechanism of the states themselves had been very considerably improved. It was not until the end of the century that this possibility became even remotely realized— that European states had paid professional armies, supplied with all they required from their own magazines, directing their activities primarily against each other and not against the civilian populations, commanded by generals who could conduct operations with restraint and skill; until the era, in fact, of those 'temperate and indecisive contests' of which Edward Gibbon was to write with such complacency in the eighteenth century.

By then two further changes had occurred in weapon technology. One was the replacement of the matchlock musket with its cumbrous and erratic loading procedure by the flint-lock, whose simple and sturdy mechanism made possible a discharge of three rounds a minute and the establishment of three ranks, capable of simultaneous fire, as the normal infantry formation. The other was the invention of the ring bayonet which, by making every infantryman his own pike-man, made it possible to eliminate pikes from the battlefield altogether. These two developments occurred during the last two decades of the seventeenth century; so the soldiers who fought under Marlborough at the beginning of the eighteenth century did so with virtually the same weapons as those available to Wellington a hundred years later, deploying in the same long thin lines—*l'ordre mince*, as the French called it —capable of sustained, continuous fire and, so long as they held their ground, invulnerable to cavalry attack.

But once these formations were broken by hostile fire, infantry were at the mercy of cavalry. So heavy cavalry armed with sword or sabre or—an importation from eastern Europe —lances, remained an effective arm. And it was from eastern Europe that there came, by way of the Habsburg armies, light cavalry for skirmishing and reconnaissance, always necessary in the wars against the Turks; while mobile fire power was provided by 'dragoons', horsemen so named after the light musket with which they were armed, and who could also be used, as their name implies, for internal coercion.

As for guns, the process of their improvement after Gustavus Adolphus was very gradual until the eighteenth century, when the French once again took the lead. Under the supervision of the Inspector of Artillery, Jean-Baptiste de Gribeauval (1715– 89), artillery pieces became standardized, their parts were made interchangeable, improvement in charges increased the range and gunsights the accuracy of fire, and lighter carriages, by greatly reducing the draught power needed to move them, made them truly flexible weapons both on and off the battle-field, capable of concentration against any desired point. But more important than any technical development was that which occurred among the gunners themselves. They ceased to be regarded as a group of civilian specialists concerned only with the obscure technicalities of their sinister craft, and became in all European armies an integrated branch of the armed forces, uniformed and disciplined like all the rest if somewhat more scientific in their approach to war. One of the prize artillery cadets at the Ecole Militaire of Brienne was to be a young Corsican, Napoleon Bonaparte.

Developments in weapon technology alone do not provide an adequate explanation of the change which came over European warfare between the time of Gustavus Adolphus and that of Frederick the Great. The really significant changes took place, not in the tools with which the armies operated, but in the structure of the armies themselves and of the states which employed them. Indeed it is doubtful whether the improvements in weapons would have taken place at all, much less have been fully exploited, if full-time professionals had not been available to put them to good effect and—perhaps more important—full-time state officials had not been in a position to take decisions about their development, arrange for their manufacture and supply, and pay for them.

The pioneer in all this was France. It was the Bourbon monarchy that took the blueprint provided by Gustavus Adolphus and developed, by the end of the century a fully functioning military mechanism which every state in Europe had to imitate if it was not to be overwhelmed by it.

When Gustavus died in 1631 it hardly appeared possible that France, her monarchy bankrupt, her society barely recovered from half a century of civil war, could ever take the lead in Europe again. In terms of European politics France was almost a nonentity. Such recovery as had been achieved was due to the success of Henry IV in bringing her civil wars to an end and to Richelieu in steering clear of foreign conflicts; or, if this was not possible, fighting them by proxy. On the death of Gustavus, who was the greatest proxy of them all, Richelieu saw himself faced with the necessity of improvising an army and entering the field himself if Habsburg power, Spanish and Austrian, was not to become dominant in Europe.

It was an appalling undertaking. The French crown had little control over the heterogeneous provinces which it ruled. It commanded only the nominal allegiance of the quarrelsome grandees whose independent habits had become during the civil wars almost ineradicable. It possessed no civil service, and most important of all, it had no money. Such money as could be made available—and throughout the Thirty Years War it

was never enough for more than about 12,000 men had to go
as lump sums to colonels who raised their own regiments, had
full responsibility for paying and equipping them, and who as
a matter of course cheated both their employers and the men
under their command; so that even the tiny forces the French
could put in the field continually melted away for lack of pay.
Senior officers were aristocrats reluctant to acknowledge any
allegiance to the Crown, refused to serve under each others'
command and conducted their quarrels flamboyantly in
public and on occasion on the battlefield itself. The action of
the most eminent of all, the Prince de Condé, who at the height
of the war transferred his services from the king of France to
the king of Spain, was exceptional, but behaviour of this kind
was not regarded as in any way odd or even reprehensible.
Inconvenient as it might be, that was the way in which the
truly great nobility might be expected to behave.

Bankruptcy, indiscipline, and corruption: these were the
characteristics of French armies, as of most others, before 1648
—indeed before Louis XIV came to the throne in 1660. Yet,
by 1680 the French forces were nearly 300,000 strong and the
wonder of Europe. A few years later they were to hold their
own with brilliance and devotion for a quarter of a century
against a coalition embracing every major European power.
How was this done?

Basically it was the work of two outstanding and tireless
bureaucrats, Michel le Tellier, who laid the foundations of the
work in the 1640s and 50s, and his son the Marquis de
Louvois who continued it under Louis XIV. Their achievement was never complete: their careers consisted of continual
attacks on abuses they could never entirely overcome and
many of which reappeared in full strength after their death.
Still, by 1700 royal control had been effectively asserted; and
instead of a congeries of independent, uncontrollable, inefficient units there had come into being a disciplined and
articulated body with a single centralized administration
capable of putting several hundreds of thousands of men into
the field and keeping them there for years.

Of course a complete explanation of their success would
have to take account of the growing wealth of the French

community, so lovingly fostered by Colbert; the improvement in its agriculture and industries, in its internal and external commerce, and in the development of a fiscal system capable of tapping this through effective taxation and excise. But money by itself could not improve military efficiency. Indeed unless military administration was improved, more money would have simply stuck in larger quantities to the fingers of the regimental colonels and the contractors who supplied the army's material needs. Le Tellier and Louvois left these colonels as the operative agents, the men who did the work of raising and paying the regiments and bearing all the financial risk which that involved; but they inspected the finished product to make quite sure that the men for whose pay the colonels indented were really there; and they removed from the control of the regimental colonels responsibility both for equipment and supply and for the conduct of operations. The crown appointed the lieutenant-colonels who commanded the regiments in the field, and the general officers who commanded the higher formations. Insubordination among these officers was punished by loss of the royal commission, and the few aristocratic commanders who tried to avoid this indignity by resigning before they could be dismissed were sent to the Bastille for *lèse-majesté*. Officers had to serve as musketeers in the royal Guard before being commissioned at all; and standards of drill, discipline, and training throughout the infantry were set by a model regiment. The colonel of that regiment acted as Inspector General for the army as a whole and his reputation has disagreeably enriched the vocabularies of both the French and the English tongues: M. de Martinet.

But the most important innovation of all was the creation of a civil bureaucracy to administer the army—a remarkable achievement considering that in those days no formal bureaucracies existed to administer anything. The crown normally either sold offices outright for ready cash, or placed contracts with individuals or syndicates for anything it wanted done; whether it was raising taxes, raising or supplying armed forces, manufacturing weapons, or as we saw in the last chapter, fitting out privateers to distress the king's enemies. This bureaucracy, the *intendance*, originated in the days of Richelieu as a regular system of inspectors or overseers visiting or residing with the armies, checking on recruiting, ensuring so far as possible regular supplies of food, ammunition, and money and reporting back to the Secretary of State for War. Le Tellier expanded this into a complete administrative framework which was put to use by his son. These officials negotiated and supervised all contracts for food, arms, and equipment— including *uniforms*, an obvious and indeed unavoidable development once the state undertook the responsibility of providing clothing on such a large scale. They divided France into areas whose economic potential was assessed and apportioned, where the feeding and billetting of troops was closely organized and where permanent magazines and arsenals were set up. Every two months they visited each regiment, investigating their strength, their commissariat, and their pay. On campaigns they accompanied the armies, organizing supply from magazines where possible and by local requisition where it was not. Disagreeable as local inhabitants found these official requisitions, they were a great deal better than the soldiers being left to forage for themselves. The *intendants* were understandably detested at every level of the army, from the senior commanders whose pride they offended to the junior officers whose accounts they checked. But it was no use complaining: behind them stood the energetic and implacable Louvois and behind him, supporting him against the expostulations of senior officers and the abuses of junior, was the king.

We must not overestimate the achievements of the *intendants*. The efficiency of the French armies must be judged against the standards of their times, not of ours. The great Sebastian Le Prestre de Vauban, whose work in providing France with a complete system of fortifications covering her frontiers was as remarkable as the achievement of Louvois in providing her with an army, wrote towards the end of the century that when he considered the condition of the French troops, 'housed like swine, half-naked, dying of hunger' he trembled for the monarchy. The will of a single powerful man, or even a group of powerful men, could not overcome difficulties which were to stretch to the limit the administrative expertise of the great bureaucracies of the nineteenth century.

Corruption still flourished, supply systems still broke down, and when they did the people who suffered were the unfortunate peasants and townspeople on whom the troops found themselves billetted. Further, as Europe became more orderly and prosperous, and as more numerous and attractive careers presented themselves in agriculture, commerce, the crafts, and the professions, it became more difficult to recruit into the ranks of the armies anyone except social drop-outs, criminals, dupes, and half-wits who could only be kept under control by ferocious discipline and who when the opportunity presented itself were liable to behave with quite bestial savagery. We must not be deceived by the superficial elegance of the armies of the rococo age: they were brutal and squalid institutions, and war was still, for those involved in it, a brutal and terrifying affair.

But with all its imperfections the French Army was the most remarkable instrument of state power that Europe had yet seen. The military institutions described above were copied with local variants by all the other states of western Europe, Britain not excepted, in much the same way as was French architecture, French art, French fashions, French court protocol, and French cuisine. The princelings of Germany, whose armies were often their most marketable asset, aped the French military example with dedicated precision; and none did so more seriously or more successfully than did the rulers of that barren, impoverished, and politically insignificant Electorate of Brandenburg, whose loyalty to the Emperor gained them, at the beginning of the eighteenth century, the title of Kings of Prussia.

It is not easy for us, looking back after a century of German triumph and tragedy, to appreciate from what a position of total weakness the Hohenzollerns began their long climb to world power. The French monarchy may have appeared weak enough at the beginning of the seventeenth century but at least its lands were compact and fertile. Those of the Electorate of Brandenburg, stitched together by a random process of inheritance, sprawling discontinuously and defencelessly across the German plain from the Vistula to the Rhine, could not compare in terms of natural wealth even with the neighbouring

lands of Saxony and Bavaria, let alone in terms of commercial
growth-potential with the United Provinces and the free cities
of the Hanseatic League. Strategically they linked those two
storm-centres of Europe, the Rhineland and the Baltic, and
even if one was peaceful hostilities were almost certainly
threatening in the other. Moreover they contained some of the
most stubbornly independent towns and insubordinate
nobility in Europe. It was difficult enough to persuade the
suspicious representatives of these Estates to provide money
for forces even for local defence, let alone for conflicts which
the Elector might have to fight at the other end of his domains.
Whatever they did, it might have been confidently predicted
that the Hohenzollerns simply could not win; against their
own subjects, let alone anyone else.

In retrospect the measures which the Great Elector Frederick
William took to overcome these difficulties seem evidence of
brilliant and unscrupulous long-term planning. In fact they
were, as is so often the case, improvisations dictated by immediate need. In 1653, at the outset of one of those Baltic wars
in which the northern and eastern lands of his Electorate were
involved, he secured from all his Estates a small grant to raise
an army a few thousand strong in return for the confirmation
of all existing privileges. The nobility were given full jurisdiction and security within their lands and a guarantee of
preferment in both secular and ecclesiastical office; the towns
were confirmed in all their judicial immunities and guild
restrictions. But the Estates were prevailed upon to agree to
the introduction of royal officials throughout the land to assess
and levy the tax required to make up their contributions for
the army—the *Generalkriegskommissariat*. So they forfeited, in
this essential particular, their traditional right—the real
guarantee of their independence—to tax themselves. They
lived to regret it.

This grant, of course, did not produce nearly enough for the
growing needs of the war, and the following year the Elector
had to take further action. In 1654 the Imperial Diet, the
representative body of the Holy Roman Empire of whose
pronouncements the German princes normally took as much
notice as do sovereign states today of the resolutions of the

General Assembly of the United Nations, urged that 'the inhabitants, subjects and citizens of every State in the Empire should obediently lend assistance to their princes, lords and superiors, to occupy and guard fortresses and other necessary places'. This anodyne recommendation was taken by Frederick William to empower him to compel his subjects to subscribe 'everything that can be asked of them for the present and future security, peace and tranquillity of the country'.[3] And the combination of this shadowy legal sanction, his new bureaucracy and a small army, gave him all the machinery he needed for raising a larger force. When in 1655 his central and eastern lands, Brandenburg and Cleves, refused to contribute to a Baltic War which they considered to be no concern of theirs, he used this army to levy taxes by force and then to establish them on a continuing basis. Eight years later when the Estates of Prussia attempted the same thing, refusing to contribute to the defences of the Rhineland territories of the Electorate when hostilities loomed between the United Provinces and France, they also were dragooned into submission. They were dragooned the more easily in that the nobility, their natural leaders, were exempt from the contribution: the bourgeoisie and the peasantry had to divide it between them. Thanks to these measures Frederick William raised an army which by 1678 was 45,000 strong and which remained at this level throughout his reign and that of his successor: not a spectacular size, but enough to achieve his purpose in making Brandenburg-Prussia a force to be reckoned with in an international community where the only ultimate sanction was military power.

It was a force large enough, also, to impose a considerable strain on a society of only some two million inhabitants with few natural sources of wealth. The royal bureaucracy responsible for levying the contributions to support this army found themselves involved in doing a good deal more. In the towns, where the money was found by an excise on goods, they extended their control over all the industrial and commercial activities. In the countryside they exercised a similar supervision over harvests, rents, and general taxation. Like the French *intendance*, these Prussian officials, the *steuerkommissäre* and *landräthe*, created a bureaucratic framework which gave the crown a new degree of control over the economic activities and resources of its subjects and which, gradually eliminating local rights and particularism, produced an effective central government focused on Berlin. A State, in fact: the Prussian State; called into being to provide for the needs of the King of Prussia's army.

Thanks to these securely laid foundations it was possible for the Great Elector's grandson King Frederick William I (1713–40) to build up an army 80,000 men strong, the fourth largest in Europe. It was organized with infinite care to impose the least possible strain on the fragile economy of his lands. The bourgeoisie, good fruitful taxpayers, did not serve at all. The ranks were recruited so far as possible from foreigners and from peasants who were sent back to their farms at seed-time and harvest; they were paid a pittance and encouraged to supplement their pay by practising a trade in their barracks; and they were of course far too precious to be allowed to do any very serious fighting. The officers were found almost exclusively from the nobility, who were virtually conscripted to the royal service—noble families being compelled to send at least one son into the cadet corps from which the mainstream of officers was drawn. In return for a confirmation of all their privileges, the Prussian nobility were bound to the services of the crown. Within a couple of generations a *noblesse* which had rivalled their neighbours the Poles in their wild and unbiddable independence had become the docile pillars of the Hohenzollern monarchy, and so remained—the von Alvenslebens, the von Tresckows, the von Falkensteins, the von Manteuffels, the von Kleists—until that monarchy collapsed two hundred years later.

The Prussian officer corps was probably the most socially exclusive in Europe, and the Hohenzollerns kept it so; partly in fulfilment of what we would now term a social compact, partly because they placed particular reliance on the aristocratic code of honour and loyalty in ensuring both courage on the battlefield and obedience to the royal command. In France the nobility had a harder time asserting their prior claims to officers' commissions. The Bourbons, like other European monarchs, emasculated the political independence of the aristocracy, the *noblesse de l'épée*, by providing them with jobs at court, in the army, and in the Church; but they considered an even more important qualification than noble lineage for the colonel of a regiment to be a full purse. So wealthy bourgeoisie were able to purchase social mobility with a commission, and they set a life-style with which the poor provincial *noblesse*, the equivalent of the Prussian *junkers*, were quite unable to keep up. The upper ranks of the French army in the eighteenth century thus became choked with the sons of well-to-do *rôturiers* and fashionable court families while the keen young nobles whose parents had neither wealth nor influence found promotion barred to them. Many, as a result, became increasingly alienated from the régime, looked longingly at the example of Spartan yet aristocratic efficiency provided beyond the Rhine and even at the yet more exciting modes of warfare which after 1776 appeared to be developing beyond the Atlantic.

Still, whether one looks at the opulent officer corps of France or the poor, arrogant, dedicated *junkers* of Prussia, or any of the intermediate examples which developed in lesser European states, the common characteristics outnumber the differences. The easy camaraderie of the old mercenaries, when seniority went with experience and young nobles trailed a pike or bore a musket with the ordinary soldiers of fortune, had given place to a rigidly hierarchial structure sharply divided between 'commissioned officers', who stood in a direct and personal relationship to the crown and who, whether they were born to it or not, adopted an aristocratic life style; and 'other ranks' regarded as a different order of being altogether, recruited from all over Europe by impressment or bounty, kept in order by a watchdog class of non-commissioned officers, disciplined by copious application of the lash and drilled until they were able even on the battlefield to perform like automata the elaborate evolutions which alone gave mobility to their long unwieldy lines, or—even more important—to stand immobile for hours while the enemy blazed away at them from point-blank range.

Battles indeed were so destructive, and professional soldiers so difficult to replace, that generals in the eighteenth century displayed the same reluctance to engage in them as had their mercenary predecessors two centuries earlier. Marshal Saxe in his *Rêveries de Guerre* (1732) made the much quoted statement: 'I do not favour pitched battles, especially at the beginning of a war, and I am convinced that a skilful general could make war all his life without being forced into one'. It was a view with which Frederick the Great in his *Instructions for his Generals* of 1747 expressed sympathy. 'The greatest secret of war and the masterpiece of a skilful general is to starve his enemy. Hunger exhausts men more surely than courage, and you will succeed with less risk than by fighting. But', he went on, 'since it is very rare that a war is ended by the capture of a depot and matters are only decided by great battles, it is necessary to use all these means to attain this object'. Indeed, he wrote, 'War is decided only by battles and is not finished except by them. Thus they have to be fought, but it should be opportunely and with all the advantages on your side .... The occasions that can be procured are when you cut the enemy off from his supplies and when you choose favourable terrain'.[4]

These quotations indicate something of the nature, problems, and objectives of eighteenth-century strategy. The problem of keeping an army some 70,000 strong provided with a continuous flow of food, fodder, and ammunition as it moved through hostile country was the first which the general had to learn to master, and many never got beyond that. No campaign could be opened until sufficient supplies for the season had been accumulated in the frontier fortresses; and since fodder for horses and mules consituted a major need of armies on the move, no move could be made until the end of the spring. The speed of any advance was then limited not only by the distances which heavily-laden troops could be expected to march over bad roads in a single day, but by the rate at which magazines could be built up along the lines of communication in their rear and the time which supply convoys took to move from base to magazine and from magazine to the front. It is indeed at this time that such expressions as *base, flanks, lines of communication, interior* and *exterior lines* began to enter the military vocabulary.

Within a few days at most the advancing army would come

upon an enemy fortress, and the commander had to decide to bypass it or to besiege it. A siege might take all summer; but to leave the fortress in his rear, a constant threat to his communications, was out of the question unless he detached enough forces to 'mask' it. A few such detachments left his main force weakened and at the mercy of the enemy army. Only a daring commander who carefully calculated the risks involved and trained his troops to rapid marching could hope for decisive results within the few months at his disposal before the autumn rains made the roads impassable. Most thought themselves lucky if they could conduct one or two successful sieges and win a favourable position from which to begin their campaign the following year. To pile up such minor successes until their aggregated weight and financial exhaustion compelled the adversary to make peace seemed preferable to staking all on a battle in which advantages accumulated over several years might be thrown away in as many hours; especially since the political objectives for which the wars were fought were seldom such as to justify such bloody solutions.

Armies in Europe by the later eighteenth century thus concerned themselves predominantly with problems of siege-craft, fortification, marches, and supply; on all of which subjects an enormous literature proliferated. They became, in Clausewitz's words, like 'a State within a State, in which the element of violence gradually faded away'. Most of their time was passed in profoundest peace. Even during wartime they campaigned for only four or five months of the year. To the outside world they were symbols of state power. For themselves they were a self-contained universe, a sub-culture with its own routine, its own ceremonies, its own music and dress and habits; that whole tedious but obsessive way of life known as 'soldiering' which has survived in the British army down to our own day. In their activities, either in war or in peace, the rest of the community took little interest, and was not encouraged to do so. Even in England, where popular support was as great as anywhere for wars, especially maritime wars, which enriched the community and involved only a minute proportion of the population, Laurence Sterne could get as far as Paris on his Sentimental Journey before anyone reminded him that, since Britain and France were at war, he ought to equip himself with a passport. On the Continent commerce, travel, cultural and learned intercourse went on in wartime almost unhindered. The wars were the king's wars. The rôle of the good citizen was to pay his taxes, and sound political economy dictated that he should be left alone to make the money out of which to pay those taxes. He was required neither to participate in making the decision out of which wars arose nor to take part in them once they broke out, unless prompted by a spirit of youthful adventure. These matters were *arcana regni*, the concern of the sovereign alone.

It might be suggested that it was not the least achievement of European civilization to have reduced the wolf packs which had preyed on the defenceless peoples of Europe for so many centuries to the condition of trained and obedient gun dogs— almost, in some cases, performing poodles. Yet this very success bred a reaction. As the wealth of Europe developed, so did the prosperity and self-confidence of a bourgeoisie which regarded this military element in their societies, with its aristocratic officers and outcast soldiery, with a total lack of sympathy: at best as a group of specialists whose affairs were no concern of theirs, at worst as an object of derision and contempt. The men of the Enlightenment no longer accepted war as the necessary destiny of mankind, a fate to be endured with patience and courage; nor did eighteenth-century economists see in it that unique source of wealth which had seemed so obvious and necessary to their seventeenth-century predecessors. Wealth was increasingly believed to derive from free and unhindered commerce in those commodities which a beneficent providence had distributed so wisely over the face of the world that men would, in exchanging them, be ever increasingly bound together by bonds of harmony and peace. So taught the physiocrats in France and the disciples of the great Adam Smith in England. War was the result of mistaken laws, false perceptions, and vested interests, and if the world was ruled and organized by clear-sighted men who understood the true nature of human and social behaviour, it need never occur. So taught Voltaire and the Encyclopaedists. For them soldiers were survivors from a bygone epoch, representatives of a life-style from which enlightened men were emancipating themselves and from which one day, soon, mankind would escape altogether.

This was one reaction to the growth of professional armies. But there was another of a very different kind. There were also those in France who saw these tightly-knit institutions, kept apart from the rest of society and reducing the conduct of war to an ever more specialized and abstruse science, as inadequate instruments for the great social and political forces which were beginning to gather momentum under the placid surface of late eighteenth-century society; forces which must find expression in new kinds of military organization, new styles of war. One of their spokesmen was the Comte Jacques de Guibert, whose *Essai générale de tactique* was published in 1772 and opened with a scathing attack on the contemporary conduct of war.

We open our campaigns with armies that are neither adequately recruited nor properly paid. Whether they win or lose, both sides are equally exhausted. The National Debt increases, credit sinks, money runs out. Navies can find no more sailors, armies no more soldiers. Ministers on each side feel it time to negotiate. Peace is made. A few colonies or provinces change hands. Often the cause of the conflict remains unresolved and each party remains sitting among its ruins and busies itself with paying off its debts and sharpening its weapons.

But suppose that there should arise in Europe a people vigorous in its genius, its resources and its government; a people in whom austere virtues and a national militia were joined to a settled policy of aggrandisement; one which did not lose sight of its purpose, which knew how to make war cheaply and to subsist on its victories, and was not reduced to laying down its arms through financial need. We would see such a people subjugate its neighbours and overthrow their feeble constitutions as the north wind shakes the tender reeds.[5]

Guibert saw no prospect of this happening. 'Such a people will not arise', he went on sadly, 'because there is no longer in Europe any nation at once powerful and new. They are all growing alike and corrupting each other'. Guibert died in 1791; a year too soon to see his remarkable prophecy beginning to come true.

5

The Wars of the Revolution

In the last decade of the eighteenth century the framework of European society, social, economic, political, and military, was shaken to its foundations. Eighteenth-century Europe was a system of states whose frontiers were clearly delineated and whose rulers were absolute sovereigns within their own realms. Their mutual relations were conducted by a precise diplomatic protocol according to clear principles of international law. Their wars were conducted with equally well-defined protocol by professional and armed forces recruited from all over Europe and officered by an almost equally international aristocratic cousinage. All this was now to be called in question and, in places, transformed. This transformation was very largely the result of twenty-five years of almost uninterrupted warfare, from 1792 until 1815, between revolutionary France and her neighbours; warfare on a scale unprecedented since the barbarian invasions. But those wars were at least as much a symptom of revolutionary change as they were a cause of it.

The nature of eighteenth-century warfare was so intimately bound up with the nature of the society conducting it that a revolution in the one was bound to cause a revolution in the other. Once the state ceased to be regarded as the 'property' of dynastic princes, however hard-working and devoted to the interests of their peoples those princes might be, and became instead the instruments of powerful forces dedicated to such abstract concepts as Liberty, or Nationality, or Revolution, which enabled large numbers of the population to see in that state the embodiment of some absolute Good for which no price was too high, no sacrifice too great to pay; then the 'temperate and indecisive contests' of the rococo age appeared as absurd anachronisms. As Carl von Clausewitz, who lived through this period, discerned, wars are not discrete entities but the expressions of state policy, the implementation of that policy by other means. As states change their nature, so will their policy change, and so will their wars.

If we consider the French armies which shattered the old system and established, however briefly, a new Carolingian Empire reaching from the Vistula to the Atlantic, we find no novel weapons to explain their achievement. Napoleon's armaments were almost identical with those of Frederick the Great. There were some important tactical innovations, but none that had not been widely discussed and to some extent practised by military theorists and commanders for decades before the revolutionary wars. Of these innovations one can pick out four: the articulation of armies into autonomous *divisions* which, since they could move along several roads simultaneously, gave greater speed and flexibility to military movement; the employment of free-moving, free-firing skir-mishers—'light' infantry or riflemen; a more flexible use of artillery on the battlefield to gain a superiority of fire at a given point; and the use of the column of attack instead of the line, a formation which emphasized offensive shock rather than defensive fire: the change from *l'ordre mince* to *l'ordre profonde*.

The first two of these developments had been made possible by the improvement of infantry weapons, but that improve-ment had occurred as long ago as the end of the seventeenth century. The flintlock musket and bayonet then introduced gave to the individual infantryman a much greater independent capacity both for delivering fire and for defending himself, and it became possible for small groups armed with these weapons to be detached from the main body as advance, rear, or flank guards; detachments which could hold their own even against superior forces until they could be relieved or withdrawn. By the mid-century such detachment for a *guerre des postes* had become commonplace, but it was not until after the Seven Years War that the French general Pierre de Bourcet suggested that the entire army might be organized along these lines. Instead of the army moving in a single block with outlying detachments Bourcet proposed, in his *Principes de la Guerre des*

Montagnes (1775) the splitting of the force into autonomous 'divisions' of all arms, each moving along its own line of advance, mutually supporting but each capable of sustained action. This would make possible not only far greater speed of movement but new flexibility of manoeuvre.

So a new kind of strategic calculation had now to be added to the traditional sciences of siegecraft and supply; one based on the speed with which divisions could come to one anothers' aid and the length of time units of different strength could be expected to resist on their own. And there was a further advantage to this kind of deployment. Small units moving along by-roads did not have to depend entirely on their lines of supply but could to some extent subsist off the country, which made their movements more rapid still. And as in the prosperous western Europe of the later eighteenth century road systems were improved and more land was brought under cultivation, the opportunities for such movement of armies increased.

As the *guerre des postes*, small-scale skirmishing in woods and villages on the fringes of the main military forces, became more general in eighteenth-century warfare, so the need developed for specialists to undertake it. Action of this kind required a self-reliance, a quick-wittedness, and a reliability which was rarely to be found among troops conditioned to fight in line under the watchful eye of their officers. The army where these talents most abounded, as a result of their long campaigns against the Turks in south-east Europe, was that of the Habsburg Empire. For the defence of their frontiers the Imperial Army has recruited local talent of a unique kind: Croatian *pandours*, Hungarian *huszars*, and Albanian *stradiots*, mainly light cavalry to scout and raid. When in 1741 the Empress Maria Theresa had to defend her western lands against the depredations of Prussia and France in the War of the Austrian Succession, she used these forces to very good effect. Her adversaries complained that these light troops, operating independently far ahead and on the flanks of the main Imperial armies, were no more than brigands and murderers, but they had to take steps to counter them. So both the French and the Prussian armies began to recruit special battalions of *chasseurs* or *jägers*, huntsmen used to stalking game in broken ground, who could fight in mountains or forests. Frederick the Great recruited his own *huszars* and, very much against his will, established *Freibattailonen* to conduct the *guerre des postes*; although he dismissed them contemptuously as 'Adventurers, Deserters and Vagabonds who were distinguished from the regular infantry only by the lack of what made the infantry strong, namely, Discipline'. Another school for skirmishers was the forests of North America where British, French, and American troops alike learned the limited value of regular European tactics and where 'irregular' warfare proliferated. By the eve of the Revolutionary Wars light infantry formations of various kinds, often clad in the distinctive huntsman's green for camouflage, were an accepted part of all European armies.[1]

As for artillery, something has already been said about the reforms introduced in the French Army in the 1760s by Jean-Baptiste de Gribeauval which made French guns standardized, mobile, and accurate. Their actual mode of employment on the battlefield was analyzed by the Chevalier Jean du Teil who with his brother, the Baron Joseph du Teil, was to be one of the patrons and teachers of the young Napoleon Bonaparte. In his work *De l'usage de l'artillerie nouvelle dans la guerre de campagne* (1778) du Teil showed how concepts familiar in siege warfare could be employed on the battlefield; in particular, how gunfire could be concentrated to make and exploit a breach in the enemy line of battle. He stressed tactical elements such as the interdependence of fire and movement and the advantage of oblique over direct fire, but always he came back to the need for concentration of effort. 'We must collect the greatest number of troops and a greater quantity of artillery at the point where we wish to break the enemy. . . . We must multiply our artillery on the points of attack which must decide the victory. . . . Artillery, thus intelligently sustained and multiplied, brings decisive results.[2]

The desire for a decisive concentration of force to break the expensive deadlock which resulted from the confrontation of orthodox lines of battle also lay behind the advocacy, continuous in the French Army since the War of the Spanish Succession, of the employment of infantry columns of attack, *l'ordre profonde*. The French had never taken so kindly as had the Prussians to *l'ordre mince*, with its requirement for iron discipline and impeccable drill. This did indeed require an army of a very peculiar kind to perform it effectively. The leading French military writer of the early eighteenth century, the Chevalier de Folard, argued so powerfully in favour of the column of attack, a deep formation designed to maximize the power of shock rather than of fire, that his teaching remained influential in the French Army until the Revolution. Disastrous attempts to implement it during the War of the Austrian Succession, when French columns were predictably shredded to pieces by the fire of the enemy line, led to subtleties and modifications as the century wore on. The most effective were those introduced by Guibert, whose flexible *ordre mixte* of small battalion-columns deploying when necessary into line became the basis of the French Army Regulations of 1791 and at least the formal doctrine of the armies of the Revolution.

But when the Revolution had to defend itself, in 1792, against the invading armies of its adversaries, there was little chance to practice formal military doctrines. Only part of the old royal army remained loyal to the revolutionary government, and that part was considered unreliable. Drilled, disciplined infantry was no longer available in sufficient quantity to practise the tactics of the *ancien régime*. The gaps in its ranks had to be filled by volunteers who had no intention of accepting the traditional discipline even if there had been time to inculcate it. So the revolutionary armies made a virtue of necessity, elevating the Rousseau-ite concept of 'the natural man' to a guiding principle and turning their backs on the artificiality of the old order. They were fighting as free men to defend freedom, and for free men a combination of individual skirmishing and mass column of attack to cries of *à la baionnette*! was the natural mode of fighting. Indeed it was the only possible mode of fighting for troops who had only handled a musket for the first time a day or two before the battle, and it did not work at all badly. One must not forget that the revolutionary armies contained a substantial stiffening of regulars, NCOs, and young officers who welcomed responsibilities and opportunities denied them under the old order, and nowhere was this more true than among the artillery and light infantry units which were so unfashionable among the court aristocracy. It was the regular artillery of the old army that fired the cannonade at Valmy in September 1792 which saved the Revolution. The following year the French Army was reconstituted as a formal *amalgame* of the old order and the new, one regular battalion being brigaded with two of volunteers, and the white of the old royal uniform took its place in the tricolour between the red and the blue of the new National Guard. The secret of the success of the new French armies was to lie in the combination of the professionalism of the *ancien régime* with the enthusiasm of a Nation in Arms.

These units might not have fought as well as they did, and they certainly would not have fought for so long as they did, if they had not been organized in the first instance by a fanatically totalitarian régime and then led by the greatest military genius the world had seen since Alexander the Great. And they would certainly not have survived the first few years of the revolutionary wars, let alone survived them victoriously, if they had not been able to counter the professional efficiency of their enemies with a great superiority in numbers. The monarchies of the *ancien régime* had to calculate their military budgets very carefully: the upkeep of regular forces was a heavy charge on their treasuries. But for a revolutionary nation, numbers were no object. By 1793 the supply of volunteers had run out, so the Law of August 23rd decreed that 'From this day until that when our enemies have been chased off the territories of the Republic, all Frenchmen are on permanent requisition for military service'. The enemy were cleared off French territory within twelve months, but conscripts were levied with increasing ruthlessness for another twenty years. By the end of 1794 Lazare Carnot, the organizer of the French revolutionary armies, had over a million men under arms, and he used them to obtain a crushing numerical superiority on every battlefield. *Agir toujours en masse*! was his watchword: 'No more manoeuvres, no more military art but fire, steel and patriotism!' The element of sheer ferocity in war, almost lost to sight in the eighteenth century, now became dominant. 'War is a violent condition' wrote Carnot; 'One should make it *à l'outrance* or go home'. And so long as terror was the order of the day at home, so should it be, *a fortiori*, on the battlefield. 'We must exterminate', he urged; 'exterminate to the bitter end!'[3] Wars were no longer to be either temperate or inconclusive.

If men could be conscripted, so also could the resources of the nation to arm, equip, clothe, and feed them; and in order to do so Carnot and his associates attempted to create a planned war economy, based on the fear of the guillotine. All crops were requisitioned apart from those considered necessary for local consumption. A national bread was produced, *pain d'égalité*, and distributed against ration cards. A maximum price was fixed for all consumer goods. Stocks of luxuries were requisitioned for export against the importation of war materials, all foreign trade being regulated by a central commission. All transport and industrial output was nationalized and put to war needs. Evasion of the restrictions by hoarding or dealings on the black market was punished by death. The manufacture of arms, ammunition, uniforms, and equipment was organized on a national basis. Even scientists were conscripted to work on problems of metallurgy, explosives, ballistics, and other matters relevant to armament manufacture. A research laboratory was set up at Meudon which devised the first military observation balloons. A semaphore telegraph was established between Paris and the frontier. For the first time science was applied to warfare on a national scale.

The performance did not live up to the concept. Totalitarian government could not be enforced with the means then available against a people who, once the immediate danger of invasion was over, were no longer prepared to accept it. Once the government of Terror and Virtue under Robespierre had been overthrown, in Thermidor 1794, the business of supplying the armies reverted to private enterprise; and since the machinery of the *intendance* normally responsible for regulating such matters was quite inadequate to control activities on so gigantic a scale, corruption flourished. Army contractors became the ostentatious *nouveaux riches* of the Directory and the Empire, and the tax payers, first of France and then of

Europe, were milked to line their pockets. It was well said of the Napoleonic armies that their members fell into three categories; the senior officers, who had glory and wealth, the junior officers and men, who had glory but no wealth, and the war commissaries who had wealth but no glory.[4]

There could be no question, after 1794, of demobilizing these immense armies: to so do would have been to create chaos within France. But there could equally be no question of their subsisting on French territory. So the war which had begun as one for the defence of France and her Revolution was transformed into one first of plunder and then of conquest. The Directory did not much care where the French armies went so long as they and their generals stayed abroad. The young Bonaparte led his starving and ragged forces into Italy in 1796 with a simple promise of plunder, thereby initiating a course of conquest which acquired an impetus of its own. If we ask why Napoleon's armies were to follow him not only into Italy but to Egypt, to Germany, to Poland, and ultimately to Russia, and recognize that an increasing number of the wretched young conscripts did so because they had no alternative and would far rather have stayed at home, we find that part of the answer lies in the prospects of loot, part in the hopes of promotion on the field—for the Napoleonic armies were most effective vehicles of social mobility—and part in a quest for adventure; all of which could be summed up in the concept of *la Gloire*, Glory. With the rigid mould of the *ancien régime* broken there was no limit to what individual valour, intelligence, and good fortune could achieve. As the Duke of Wellington was to put it.

(Napoleon) was the Sovereign of the country as well as the military chief of the army. That country was constituted upon a military basis. All its institutions were framed for the purpose of forming and maintaining its armies with a view to conquest. All the offices and rewards of the State were reserved in the first instance exclusively for the army. An officer, even a private soldier, might look to the sovereignty of a kingdom as a reward for his services.[5]

The spirit of romantic heroism which inspired so much of the art of the period thus coexisted happily in the *Grande*

Armée with a more straightforward zest for loot. It was an epoch on which generations of Frenchmen, irrespective of class, were to look back with understandable nostalgia.

These were the ideas, and this the instrument, that Napoleon found to hand, and he used them with a genius that was as much political as military. Perhaps among his predecessors only Marlborough had shown a comparable capacity to visualize a campaign as a whole instead of as a series of discrete sieges and battles—to discern the object for which all military operations were conducted; whether it was, as with Piedmont in 1796, the isolation and conciliation of a wavering adversary or, as with Prussia in 1806, the total destruction and elimination of a powerful opponent. Political objectives thus dictated strategic planning; and strategic planning was directed towards discerning the decisive point in the enemy position and striking against it with irresistible force. So much Napoleon had learned from du Teil and from his own studies as an artillery cadet. 'Strategic plans are like sieges', he wrote; 'concentrate your fire against a single point. Once the breach is made, the balance is shattered and all the rest becomes useless.'[6] With numerically superior opponents the decisive point was that which divided their forces, making possible defeat in detail as happened in Italy in 1796 and very nearly happened again at Waterloo. With an inferior enemy it was the point at which his communications were most vulnerable, so that he was forced either to fight at a disadvantage or capitulate as ignominiously as did the luckless Austrian general Mack at Ulm in 1805.

This decisive concentration arose from an initial *dispersal* of forces, a deployment so wide that it was impossible to discern in advance where Napoleon intended to strike. In the four years of peace between 1801 and 1805, the only substantial breathing-space between his wars, Napoleon organized the French armies according to a pattern which was to be adopted by all European forces for the next century and a half; one which made possible almost unlimited decentralization under a single supreme command. The army was divided into army corps, each composed of two or three divisions, infantry and cavalry, of 8000 men apiece. Each division comprised two brigades, each brigade two regiments, each regiment two battalions. In 1805 these corps were quartered all over western Europe—northern France, the Netherlands, Hanover—and were brought together with perfect timing to surround the Austrian army at Ulm. Then they again dispersed, to converge on the Austrians and Russians at Austerlitz. The following year they advanced northward, spread out like beaters, to destroy the Prussians at Jena. The complex calculations involved in these movements by hundreds of thousands of men through broken country over indifferent roads, calculations which later generations established large general staffs to work out, Napoleon carried in his capacious head.

The object of these strategic manoeuvres was to bring the French armies into the best possible position to deliver battle— a battle to be looked on not as at best a necessary evil but rather as the grand climax of the entire campaign. For this Napoleon adopted and refined the tactics of the revolutionary armies. A cloud of skirmishers and sharp-shooters went ahead of the main force to disorganize the enemy resistance. Artillery raked the enemy lines; and infantry columns several thousand strong charged repeatedly and enthusiastically with the bayonet against the enemy defences until a weak point showed itself against which Napoleon could concentrate his gunfire and launch his reserves. Clumsily used against steady and well-sited regular troops like the British in the Peninsula or at Waterloo, such tactics could be suicidal. But the Prussians at Jena were no less steady and professional, and even their discipline collapsed after hours of bombardment and skirmishing fire from adversaries they could not even see. And then when the line had at last collapsed Napoleon unleashed his cavalry in a pursuit designed to complete the destruction of the enemy and the enemy state; a deep penetration to spread panic among the enemy population and destroy all hope of recovery.

But as wars continued and the quality of the conscripts deteriorated, Napoleonic tactics became little more than straightforward slogging matches. The troops raised after 1806 were taught neither to march nor to manoeuvre; barely even to fire their weapons. Such rudimentary skills as they needed

they picked up from their comrades on the march. At Aspern-
Essling in 1809 Napoleon threw his columns into battle against
the Austrians with minimal preparation, and suffered as a
result a well-deserved defeat. Thereafter he tried to make up
for the poor quality of his troops by multiplying the number
of his guns, but even so he bought his victories at the expense
of increasingly heavy casualties. Aspern was revenged at
Wagram a few days later, but Napoleon lost 30,000 men in the
process (as against 8,000 at Austerlitz). At Borodino in 1812 he
did not attempt any manoeuvres against the Russian position
but charged it head on, carrying it eventually with a loss of
30,000 men he could ill afford but entirely failing to destroy
Kutusov's army. In their clumsy battering against Wellington's
lines at Waterloo the French lost 25,000 out of 72,000 men,
over a third of their strength.

If he did not win his battle, Napoleon's entire strategy was
ruined. Although he did not ignore problems of supply, and
indeed made careful preparations at the outset of every
campaign, the speed with which he drove on his armies made
it impossible for their supply columns to keep up. They thus
had to a large extent to live off the country as had their
predecessors in the Thirty Years War. Napoleon expected his
troops to fend for themselves, which indeed they did, though
they did not make the French cause very popular in the
process. But when the size of armies ran into six figures, they
could do this only for short periods, and so long as they kept on
the move. For more prolonged subsistence they relied on
capturing the enemy's magazines after the battle and then
forcing the defeated country to support them. But when in
1807 Napoleon began to penetrate into the less fertile areas of
Europe, into Poland after the battle of Eylau, and into the
Iberian peninsula, supply became a nagging and insoluble
problem. The secret of Wellington's success in the Peninsula
lay in the cool ruthlessness with which he exploited and
exacerbated the French supply difficulties while ensuring that
he should have none of his own. The success of the Russians in
1812 rested on their ability to deny Napoleon his decisive
battle and permit him to advance into their country to a far
deeper extent than his supply arrangements could cover.

Winter and starvation did the rest. In the three years left to him Napoleon had to confine himself to operations of more traditional scope; and the traditional talents conserved by the armies of his opponents were able to show up to a better effect.

It is not to underrate the achievements of these opponents to suggest that Napoleon's downfall was brought about ultimately less through their efforts than through the weakness of his own methods—methods which made such outrageous demands on the resources of France and his own good fortune that nemesis was bound, sooner or later, to catch up with him. The success enjoyed by such cool-headed commanders of the old school as the Archduke Charles of Austria and the Duke of Wellington showed that the strategic and tactical doctrines of the eighteenth century, with their emphasis on good supply lines and solid discipline on the battlefield, still possessed enduring value. But it was equally clear that an unthinking attachment to eighteenth-century stereotypes in face of the Napoleonic methods was disastrous; and nowhere was this more clear than in the state which had brought eighteenth-century warfare to its highest peak of effectiveness, the Kingdom of Prussia.

Prussia's brief experience in the war of the First Coalition, 1792–5, and observation of Bonaparte's campaigns between 1796 and 1801 had convinced a group of young officers in the Prussian Army that they were confronting something new in warfare; that the release of national energies evident in the French Revolution was no passing phenomenon, but a fundamental change which would transform both political and military relations in European societies, and to which their own country would need to react, not only with military but with political reforms. The catastrophe of Jena in 1806 vindicated most signally the ideas of these men—Gerhard von Scharnhorst, Hermann von Boyen, August von Gneisenau, Carl von Clausewitz. Scharnhorst, their leader, was appointed President of the Military Reorganization Commission set up after Jena to remodel the Prussian Army. It was clearly not enough mechanically to imitate such French formations and techniques as the divisional system and the employment of light infantry. So long as the Prussian Army consisted of long-service conscripts despised by the rest of the population and kept in order by the lash, no serious military reform was possible. The army had to consist of serious, intelligent, reliable patriots who saw themselves as the defenders of their country and were seen as such by the rest of the community. But first it was necessary, as Gneisenau drily remarked, 'to give the People a Fatherland if they are to defend that Fatherland effectively'. And was that Fatherland simply the hereditary estates of the Hohenzollern family? Was it not rather a broader, nobler concept: Germany?

These were dangerous thoughts—the kind of thoughts, indeed, that the Hohenzollerns and the Habsburgs and their attendant nobilities considered that they were fighting France to suppress. To fight fire with this kind of fire was hardly an appealing prospect, and Scharnhorst and his collaborators found themselves faced with bitter opposition from the court and within the army itself. Some gave up in despair and, like Clausewitz, took service with the Russian Army. But in 1813, after the destruction of Napoleon's armies in Russia, the situation was transformed. An outburst of patriotic enthusiasm throughout Germany, among all classes, broke down many of the old barriers. Conscription was introduced, and a national service force, the Landwehr, was created which elected its own officers and in which service was compulsory for all men of military age who were not called up into the army itself. The army and the *landwehr* between them put into the field nearly 600,000 men, clumsy at first but implacable and courageous, who played their full part in the defeat of Napoleon at Leipzig in 1813, in the invasion of France which forced his abdication in 1814, and in his final overthrow in 1815. The Napoleonic invasions had evoked in Germany a Nation in Arms; but since that Nation could not yet find expression through the medium of any single state a major problem had been laid up for the future.

The *coup de grâce* to Napoleon at Waterloo was jointly administered by a Prussian Army commanded by Marshal Blücher and a largely British Army commanded by the Duke of Wellington, and the latter was as much the product of a military renaissance as the former. Britain's insular position

and maritime strength throughout the eighteenth century had
kept her army a small, marginal institution for whose maintenance authority had to be annually sought from a suspicious
Parliament and was sullenly granted. In peacetime it was
occupied mainly in garrisoning overseas possessions, including
the most troublesome of all, Ireland. For war new regiments
were recruited *ad hoc* and disbanded when peace came.
Regular forces of the crown were, in the words of the greatest
legal luminary of the eighteenth century, Blackstone, 'to be
looked on only as temporary excrescences bred out of the
distemper of the State, and not as any part of the permanent
and perpetual laws of the Kingdom'.[7] To defend the realm the
British governing classes looked in the first instance to the
Royal Navy and in the second to the Militia, the 'Constitutional Force' which the country gentry kept under their own
control. Mistrust of the power of a crown which had in 1688
shown every sign of intending to use a standing army to extend
its powers died only very slowly. The expansion of the army
made necessary by the revolutionary wars—from under 40,000
men in 1793 to just under 150,000 in 1801—was scrutinized
step by step by a jealous Parliament. The attempts made during
this period by its royal commander-in-chief the Duke of York
to bring it to a state of continental efficiency were attacked by
Whigs and Radicals alike. Pioneer attempts to set up a Royal
Military College for the education of officers were seen as
evidence of incipient despotism. In fact, although the army in
principle owed allegiance to the crown, the gentry retained an
effective control over it by the institution of purchase of commissions and the maintenance of a regimental system which
ensured that wealth, even on a modest scale, and social self-
selection should be the determining factor in the recruitment
of officers.

The British Army thus remained throughout the Napoleonic
wars an eighteenth-century force, faithfully reflecting the
stable class-structure of its society. Officers were drawn largely
from the lesser aristocracy and gentry, barely at all from the
professional and mercantile middle classes. Other ranks were
recruited by bounty from the marginal elements in society, and
the two existed side by side in different worlds, communicating

only through non-commissioned officers. A few leading soldiers, Sir John Moore and Sir Ralph Abercrombie foremost among them, tried to break the mould and introduce some of the flexibility and independence of the French system; but the dominant figure was Arthur Wellesley, Duke of Wellington, a man who embodied all the serene certainties of the eighteenth century and carried them into the second half of the nineteenth. Wellington saw no need for change. He was a consummate master of eighteenth-century warfare, and the limited nature of the campaigns he was required to fight made it unnecessary for him to contemplate any other. A French general of the period was reported as saying that the British infantry were the best in the world, and it was a good thing there were so few of them. But it was precisely because there were so few of them that they were so good. If the British had had to create an army on a continental scale, they would have had to take the continental model very much more seriously; which would, in its turn, have had far-reaching implications for the structure of their own society.

That they did not have to raise an army on a continental scale was due to the ascendancy established and maintained by the Royal Navy which was by the end of the eighteenth century a professional fighting force second to none in the world. This ascendancy had been challenged by the French throughout the eighteenth century. The triumphs of the Royal Navy during the Seven Years War, 1756–63, had eliminated the French as colonial rivals in North America and India; but the French Navy learned from its mistakes and twenty years later, through sheer superior professional ability, was able to inflict on the British a series of defeats which compelled the latter to renounce their attempts to repress the revolt of their American colonies.

But the Revolution destroyed the professional cadres on which the excellence of the French Navy depended, and revolutionary élan proved to be of limited effectiveness in the navigation of men-of-war. Both the command and the supply system of the French Navy disintegrated. As for the British, they reflected deeply on the faults which had led to their humiliations between 1778 and 1783. Parliament was more

generous to the navy than to the army: in the first two years
after the conclusion of peace, 1784–5, £20m, out of a total
national expenditure of £50m, was spent on restoring the navy.
The Augean Stables of Admiralty administration were cleansed
by a new Comptroller, Sir Charles Middleton. Admiral Sir
Charles Douglas introduced reforms of gunnery comparable to
those of Gribeauval in France, making naval gunfire flexible,
fast and accurate, encouraging British men-of-war to close
with and destroy their adversaries at close quarters instead of
standing off and raking them with fire.

A new signalling system gave a far greater degree of initiative, flexibility, and control to naval commanders, so this
close-quarter fighting did not result in the confusion of the old
mêlées. Already the rigid inflexibility of the line of battle, which
had dominated war at sea in the eighteenth century as completely as it had dominated war by land, had begun to break
down in the War of American Independence. Now British
admirals had the capacity to use an infinite variety of tactical
formations and expedients, and a sagacious Admiralty
encouraged them to do so. Rodney, Howe, Jarvis, above all
Nelson, showed how to combine the new techniques with
professional skill and a tactical flair which bewildered their
opponents, destroyed in succession the fleets of all their
traditional enemies the Spanish, the Dutch, the French, and
established a dominance over the oceans of the world which
was to endure well into the twentieth century.

It was this dominance, total after the Battle of Trafalgar in
1805, that enabled Britain to make a yet greater contribution
to the defeat of Napoleon: the continental blockade. In the
economic conditions of the time, when the nations of Europe
were very largely self-sufficient in foodstuffs, the reciprocal
blockades imposed on one another by the British and the
French were initially seen by both sides not, as they were to
become in the world wars of the twentieth century, attempts at
mutual starvation, but as a continuation of those 'wars of the
merchants' that we have already considered: a reversion to the
mercantilist attempts to ruin one's opponent financially by the
capture of his trade. One reason why the peace concluded in
1802 between Britain and France at Amiens was so short-lived

was that Napolcon, with conoiderable support from the French
business community, was determined to revive the Colbertian
mercantile war against British trade which had been briefly
interrupted by the Eden Treaty of 1786, that gallant attempt
by William Pitt to implement Adam Smith's principles of free
trade. Free from the internal customs barriers of the *ancien
régime*, strengthened by the acquisition of the coal and iron of
their newly annexed Belgian provinces, the French were now
dangerous competitors. Mutual blockade played a major part
in the wars of the First and Second Coalitions; France being
able, as she was between 1780 and 1783, to unite the mercantile nations of northern Europe in a League of Armed Neutra-
lity in protest against the pretensions of the British blockade.
It was thus in continuation of an established policy that in
1806, after Trafalgar had assured British control of the sea and
Austerlitz and Jena French control of the land, Napoleon
issued the Berlin Decrees, banning British and British-
controlled goods from all lands under his control.

The British response was to impose a blockade designed, not
to destroy French trade, but to control it. As a British states-
man of the time put it, 'France by her decrees has resolved to
abolish all trade with England. England said in return that
France should have no trade but with England'.[8] Neutral
vessels were permitted to trade with the French Empire only
under conditions imposed by the British—a restriction which
rapidly led to friction and ultimately in 1812 to war with the
United States. And since the continental markets were hungry
not only for such English goods as cloth and metal but for the
colonial produce—the cottons, the dyes, the sugar, the coffee
—of which she now enjoyed a total monopoly, the British
blockade was able to impose on continental Europe almost
intolerable hardships mitigated only by smuggling on a
tremendous scale—smuggling in which the French government
was compelled not only to acquiesce but even to partake.

As a result the peoples of Europe were less conscious of the
political benefits brought them by the standard-bearers of the
French Revolution than they were of the oppression and the
corruption of an inadequately controlled economy. To make
his self-imposed blockade work, Napoleon was driven to

extend his control yet further. Spain, Portugal, and Italy were forced into his 'Continental system' in 1808, thus creating support for the British throughout the Mediterranean. Holland and north Germany were brought in in 1809, Sweden in 1810, Napoleon wringing his hands and complaining that but for the British he would be able to demobilize his armies and live in peace. If by 1812 the whole of continental Europe, even France, was in a state of simmering discontent, much of the credit must go to the patient, unspectacular blockade work of the Royal Navy which its earlier victories had made possible. In that year the Czar Alexander of Russia, who had brought his country into the system five years earlier at Tilsit, decided that the interruption to his trade in timber and grain with England was intolerable, and defiantly resumed commercial relations. Napoleon saw no alternative but to reduce him to obedience by force of arms.

But there was another side to the picture. The British economy did not survive intact. War was no longer, as it had been a hundred years earlier, synonymous with trade and profit. The English merchants who captured the French colonial trade did well enough, but of far more importance now were the manufacturers whose cloth and metal-ware could not be so easily smuggled into a Europe where the market for them was still in any case limited. A crisis of glut in 1808 was temporarily alleviated by the opening of the markets of the Spanish and Portuguese Empires to British trade when Napoleon invaded the Iberian peninsula. Exports to South America rose from £8m in 1805 to nearly £20m in 1809, and a pattern of trade was established which was to last until the Second World War. But it was a mixed blessing. The feverish speculation led to a collapse of the market in 1810. At the same time the United States, retaliating against the British blockade of the continent, had boycotted British goods, and exports to Europe sank from £7·7m in 1810 to £1·5m in 1811. English warehouses were clogged with unsaleable goods, workers were laid off, rioting and machine-breaking began, and to crown the woes of the British, a series of bad harvests sent the price of bread soaring. The British Army was called out to perform the task which, far more than any foreign wars, was to keep it occupied for the next forty years: the suppression of the discontents of the British people.

So behind the spectacular military events of the revolutionary and Napoleonic eras there was taking place a struggle between two competing economic systems which was in the last resort to be no less decisive and, for the future of warfare, far more significant. War was beginning to become total—a conflict not of armies but of populations. And this trend was to be powerfully reinforced by the technical developments which, within a few years of the conclusion of the Congress of Vienna, began to transform the continent of Europe.

6

The Wars of the Nations

After 1814 the principal concern of the governing classes of Europe, settling uneasily back into the saddles from which twenty-five years of revolution and invasion had so nearly dislodged them, was to ensure that the Napoleonic experience should not be repeated; that the political and social balance which had kept eighteenth-century Europe in a state of stable equilibrium should be restored and maintained. The restoration of this balance was seen as a far more important objective than the exploitation of the new sources of political energy and military power which the French Revolution had revealed beneath the surface of European society. If military effectiveness on a Napoleonic scale depended on a revolutionary transformation of society as a whole, that was a price which the monarchs of the Restoration were not prepared to pay. Whatever value Napoleonic warfare might have for a power trying to overthrow the states-system of Europe, it could have little for statesmen trying to preserve it.

For half a century, therefore, armies reverted so far as they could to an eighteenth-century pattern of aristocratic officers and long-serving professional troops kept isolated from the rest of the community. States which had made only marginal or temporary adjustments in their military structures to meet the Napoleonic challenge—Britain, Russia, the Habsburg Empire—returned without difficulty to their traditional ways. In Prussia the reforms introduced by Scharnhorst and his colleagues and established by the Army Law of 1814—conscription for three years with the colours and two with the reserve, a separate *landwehr* officered by men of property elected by their fellows—could not be totally abolished; but the reformers themselves were cased out into obscurity or retirement, the *landwehr* was allowed to decay into a country club, conscription was used as sparingly and cautiously as possible, and the aristocracy were allowed to re-establish their total dominance within the officer-corps. In France so total a reversion to the *ancien régime* was not possible: French military institutions had to be built on the framework of the old Napoleonic army—a task undertaken by Napoleon's former lieutenants Gouvion St. Cyr in 1818 and Soult in 1832. Their military legislation retained the principle of conscription; but by applying it virtually to the only classes too poor to purchase exemption and by making it last for a period of seven years, they used it to fashion a long-serving professional army very different from the Nation in Arms of the revolutionary period. It was officered, not by aristocrats, but by professionals, who at the lower levels were largely drawn from the ranks, who had few links with the civilian world and who learned, during the frequent changes of régime that characterized French political life in the first half of the century, that their wisest course lay in unquestioning obedience to their hierarchical superiors. The French army showed itself as dependable an instrument for the defence of the social and political order as the British, the Prussian, the Austrian, and the Russian; all of which for the best part of forty years were kept far busier in repressing riot and revolution at home than in fighting, or preparing to fight, one another.

Yet the Napoleonic experience could not be ignored by armed forces whose formal *raison d'être* was the defence of their country and in consequence the waging, if necessary, of *la grande guerre*. During the course or in the aftermath of the Napoleonic wars all the major belligerent powers had established or reconstituted military schools for the professional education of officers and the training of staff officers—Britain the Royal Military College in 1802, France at St. Cyr in 1808, Prussia the *Kriegsakademie* in Berlin in 1810, Russia the Imperial Military Academy in 1832—and the lessons of the recent campaigns had to be absorbed into their curricula. Military literature, already substantial before the Revolution, became an uncontrollable flood during and after the wars as soldiers of every rank and every nation hastened to record their experiences and to pontificate about the conclusions to be drawn from them. The most respected strategists were those who emphasized the continuity between the old form of war and the new, who brought together the expertise of Napoleon and of Frederick the Great and showed the fundamental principles which, having underlain the successes of these two great Captains, could be confidently expected to hold good for the future. In the work of such men—the Prussian General von Willisen (*Theorie des grossen Krieges*, 1840), the English Edward Bruce Hamley (*Operations of War*, 1866), and above all the Swiss Antoine de Jomini (*Précis de l'Art de la Guerre*, 1838)— Napoleonic warfare became, like eighteenth-century warfare, a simple problem of manoeuvre, of threatening the enemy flanks and lines of communication while safeguarding one's own, of ensuring a superiority of strength at the decisive point. Much of the greatest military work of the time, Carl von Clausewitz's *Vom Kriege* (1832) was taken up with the same search for fundamental strategic principles; but Clausewitz was yet more concerned with analyzing and explaining the differences between the wars of the Revolution and those of the *ancien régime* than he was with stressing the similarities. War, he insisted, was at least as much a matter of moral and political factors as of military expertise, and it was the altera- tion in these factors brought about by the French Revolution that had apparently changed the nature of war and taken the armies of the *ancien régime* by surprise. Wars conducted with the full force of national energy in pursuit of total victory would always take a different form from those engaged with limited forces for limited objectives. The former category, 'absolute wars', might have seemed no more than a Platonic ideal, an abstract standard for calculation, if Europe had not actually experienced them during the revolutionary epoch. It would be rash, concluded Clausewitz, to assert that such conflicts would never recur. 'When barriers which in fact consisted only in ignorance of what was possible are broken down, it is not easy to build them up again; and mutual hostility, at least when major interests are at stake, will express itself in the same fashion as it has in our own day'.[1]

It was precisely this outburst of national enthusiasm, as dangerous to themselves as to their enemies, that the statesmen of the Restoration hoped that they would not live to see again, and for over thirty years they worked successfully to prevent it. But their very success in maintaining peace and order in Europe for so long made possible industrial and technical developments which ultimately ensured that war, when it did recur, was likely to be on a scale to dwarf even the Napoleonic experience.

It was these years between the end of the Napoleonic wars in 1815 and the war in the Crimea forty years later that witnessed the transformation of land and sea transport by the developments of the steam engine. The effect on naval warfare will be discussed in the next chapter. On land the introduction of the railway and its application to warfare eliminated the prolonged marches, lasting sometimes for weeks, which decimated even the toughest professional forces before they made contact with one another. In Britain in 1830 a regiment of troops was transported over the thirty-four miles between Manchester and Liverpool in two hours instead of taking two or three days on the march. At the same time the Germans of the Rhineland began to contemplate with apprehension the speed with which a renascent France would now be able to concentrate large bodies of troops swiftly and unexpectedly to renew the Napoleonic invasions. As it was, both the British and the French armies were initially interested in railways as a means of transporting troops to quell riots in their big cities, and it was to be the economic and military power of Prussia, whose sprawling territories in the centre of Europe could now be effectively linked together by a railway network, that was to benefit most from the new transport system.

The first war in Europe to demonstrate the value of railways was that fought between France and the Austrian Empire in northern Italy in 1859, when a French force 120,000 strong, which would have taken two months to march the distance, reached the theatre of operations in eleven days. But the campaign demonstrated also the problems of rail transport. Men and horses might be moved quickly, but their stores were a different matter. The French troops found themselves without ammunition, medical supplies, fodder, bridging, or siege equipment, and were able to fight effectively only because the Austrians were no better. The Prussian General Staff, studying with deep interest a campaign fought between its two most probable enemies, did not miss this lesson, and established a railway section which, after making its own mistakes in the war against Austria in 1866, was to function with unprecedented efficiency in the Franco-Prussian war of 1870; by which time the American Civil War had provided further lavish examples of the problems and possibilities which rail transport presented to the strategist.

Speed of movement was indeed only one of the military advantages conferred by the railway. No less important was the staying power it gave to armies in the field. No longer were armies dependent on the supplies stock-piled in forward magazines for a single campaign: now the economy of the entire country could be geared to providing a continuous supply. Secondly, troops now arrived in the theatre of operations in full strength and in good physical shape; not an unimportant consideration if any significant proportion of them were reservists fresh from civil life, although this had the incidental disadvantage that the toughening process of the approach march could no longer provide a gradual intro-duction to the rigours of the campaign. Thirdly the forces could be maintained in good condition: the sick and wounded could be evacuated to base hospitals and replaced by fit men, and if the campaign was prolonged, troops could come and go on leave. War was no longer a remote affair about which the civil population learned only from brief governmental announcements or soldiers' tales long after the event. And the intimacy of the contact between the theatre of operations and the home base was made closer by the concurrent development of the electric telegraph, which gave instantaneous com-munication, not only between political leaders in the capital and their military commanders in the field but, as newspapers became more established and ambitious, between editorial offices and their correspondents with the troops. The British public were able to follow the campaign in the Crimea in 1854–5 in far greater detail, and as a result with far greater

critical interest, than they did Wellington's campaigns in the
Peninsula; and they were only slightly less well-informed about
the activities of their armed forces in yet more remote parts of
the world.

The revolution in communication which took place during
the first half of the nineteenth century thus brought the peoples
of Europe—peoples becoming increasingly literate, urbanized,
and politically aware—into a new intimacy and involvement
with the activities of their armed forces, even though their
governments still attempted to keep these forces insulated
from a popular concern which they feared was more likely to
corrupt than to encourage them. But the same processes which
were increasing the involvement of the armed forces with the
community from which they were drawn were simultaneously
creating a purely military requirement for governments to
draw on the resources of those communities more deeply than
ever in order to sustain them.

In the eighteenth century it was generally accepted that
there was a strict limit to the size of armies that could usefully
be deployed in the field—a limit fixed by problems of supply.
Very seldom did eighteenth-century commanders operate with
armies in excess of 80,000 men. These bounds were trans-
cended, as we have seen, by the French armies of the revolutionary era, which supplemented their regular supply sources
by organized or unorganized pillage; but the disaster which
overtook the armies some 600,000 strong which Napoleon led
into Russia in 1812 showed that even this ruthless improviza-
tion had its limits. With the introduction of railways these
limits disappeared. Once the administrative complexities of
moving armies by rail were mastered, as they were mastered by
the Prussian General Staff in the 1860s, the only restrictions on
size were the numbers of men of military age in the community,
the political and economic constraints on their conscription,
and the administrative capacity to train, equip, and mobilize
them. In 1870 the North German Confederation deployed
against France exactly twice the number of men Napoleon had
led into Russia—1,200,000. By 1914 the German figure had
again doubled, to 3,400,000 men; with comparable increases
among her neighbours. By the end of the century the security

of continental powers was seen to depend primarily if not entirely on the size of the armed forces they were able to put into the field.

This assumption rested very largely on the experiences of the German Wars of Unification in 1866 and 1870, when Prussia had taken only a few weeks to destroy the armies first of the Austrian Empire and then of France and, in the latter case, to occupy the enemy capital in true Napoleonic fashion and dictate her own terms to a completely helpless foe. 'Absolute war', as predicted by Clausewitz, had appeared again; and it was brought back to Europe by Clausewitz's disciple, the Chief of the Prussian General Staff the elder Helmuth von Moltke.

The foundation for Prussian military effectiveness was the system of compulsory military service which, though it had languished since its introduction in 1814, had never been totally abandoned. It was revitalized when there came to the throne in 1858, first as Regent and then as King William I, a prince who set the revival of Prussian military power as his primary aim, and who provoked a head-on collision with his Parliament in the process. His Minister for War, Albrecht von Roon, re-established the requirement for military service as three years with the colours, four with the reserve; after which the trained soldiers passed into a *landwehr* which lost its independent status and was brought under the control of the regular army. The system was administered by regionally-based army corps whose commanders were responsible for the call-up of conscripts, reservists, and *landwehr* alike; for their training and equipment; and, most important of all, for the speed and efficiency of their mobilization. On mobilization the regular army was reinforced by fully-trained reservists, equipped from mobilization stores, and then despatched by the carefully-planned railway system to whichever frontier was selected as the main theatre of operations according to plans previously worked out by the General Staff.

This General Staff was perhaps the great military innovation of the nineteenth century. That of Prussia had been created under Scharnhorst but was entirely reorganized by Moltke when he became Chief in 1857. The problems of supplying and deploying large forces had long since made necessary the expansion of the duties of command staffs and the provision of trained if not fully-specialized staff officers in all armies. With the increase in the size of these armies brought about by the development of railways the problems both of peacetime preparation and of wartime command and control were greatly increased. In the French, Austrian, and British armies staff officers, submerged beneath their weight, became little more than military bureaucrats, out of touch with and despised by their regimental colleagues. Moltke, on the contrary, turned them into an élite, drawn from the most promising regimental officers, trained under his eye and alternating in their careers between staff and command posts of increasing responsibility. In the Prussian Army, and the army of that German Empire which was born out of the triumph of 1871, staff officers were not simply *chefs de bureau* but professional advisers whose commanders increasingly allowed themselves to be guided by their views. 1870 was as much a victory for Prussian bureaucratic method as it was for Prussian arms: it set standards of social efficiency of an entirely new kind. The romantic heroism of the Napoleonic era, which had been revived in the armies of the Second Empire and had flourished in the small colonial campaigns where most of the French generals had made their mark, was steam-rollered into oblivion by a system which made war a matter of scientific calculation, administrative planning, and professional expertise. After 1871 the Prussian institutions—conscription, strategic railways, mobilization techniques, above all the General Staff—were copied by every state in continental Europe. Thirty years later, after disastrous experiences in South Africa and Cuba, Britain and the United States adapted the model to their own needs.

Side by side with this administrative revolution went the technological. We have seen how slowly, between the fifteenth and the nineteenth centuries, weapons-systems developed within the stable economic framework of European society; the gradual, piecemeal fashion in which cannon became more mobile and slightly more accurate, the adaptations which converted matchlock into flintlock, pike into bayonet, without substantially increasing the range of fire or transcending the limits on mobility imposed by human and equine capabilities. But between 1815 and 1914, as the revolution in communications was to transform strategy, so the revolution in weapons technology was to transform tactics.

Already by 1870 firearms had undergone one transformation. First came rifling—the spiral grooves on the inside of the barrel which increased both range and accuracy by a factor of about five. The principle had been applied to sporting guns since the sixteenth century and rifles had been used by light infantry specialists since the eighteenth. But loading them at the muzzle made for a very slow rate of fire; they were generally regarded as weapons of precision too delicate for general issue, and sheer volume of fire was considered more important in the infantry line than either range or accuracy. But in the 1840s rifled muskets were developed whose bullets could be dropped down the barrel and on being fired expanded to fit the grooves, giving a rate of fire similar to that of the old musket with added range and accuracy as well. Simultaneously the flintlock firing mechanism was replaced by the far more reliable percussion cap. With these weapons the French, British, Russian, and Austrian armies fought their campaigns in the Crimea and in Italy in the 1850s.

In these campaigns the Prussians played no part; so it was not until their war against Austria in 1866 that the effectiveness of the Dreyse 'needle gun' with which they had been equipping their infantry for the last twenty years could be gauged. This was the first rifled breech-loader—a clumsy weapon which lacked the range of the muzzle-loader and was, thanks to the massive escape of gas from the breech, very disagreeable to fire. But it fired three shots to the muzzle-loader's one, and possessed the supreme advantage that it could be fired lying down. For the first time in the history of war the infantryman could kill his adversary at a range of several hundred yards without presenting a target himself—an advantage which the Prussians put to such good effect in 1866 that all other European armies rapidly acquired improved breech-loaders of their own.

In artillery the same development took place. By 1860 all European armies were equipped with various kinds of muzzle-

loading rifled cannon with ranges of between one thousand
and three thousand yards. Here the Prussian army lagged
behind both the Austrian and the French; but the indifferent
performance of their guns in 1866 led to a rapid revolution in
their tactics and the introduction of the new steel breech-
loading cannon developed by Friedrich Krupp. These guns
dominated the battlefields of 1870. After the first checks
inflicted on German forces by the superior French *chassepot*
rifles, the Prussian generals kept their infantry out of range and
used their guns to batter the French armies into submission.

Already by 1870, therefore, it was becoming difficult for an
attacking force to close with the enemy. Prussian infantry
assaulting French positions and French cavalry attacking
Prussian positions suffered horribly. Prussian victories in the
field were due partly to their artillery and partly to the outflanking tactics made possible by their superiority in numbers.
After 1870 this difficulty was to be yet further increased. The
1880s saw the development of high explosives—lyddite, cordite,
melinite: materials which, unlike gunpowder, combusted
totally and instaneously, making no smoke to betray the
position of the firer, leaving little deposit in the barrel to slow
down the rate of fire, and increasing the range of all weapons
to a hitherto inconceivable extent. Infantry rifles could now be
made effective up to a thousand yards. Their calibre could be
reduced, rendering them lighter and more accurate and
making it possible for infantrymen to carry more ammunition.
Magazines and metal cartridges improved the ease and rapidity
of loading. And the performance of even these improved
weapons was to be dwarfed by the introduction, towards the
end of the century, of belt-fed, water-cooled machine-guns,
firing several hundred rounds a minute. How could positions
defended by such weapons possibly be assaulted?

Tactical writers at the close of the century all agreed that the
attack could succeed only by developing a greater intensity of
fire than the defence. Concurrent developments in artillery
made this appear possible. Increased ranges meant that field-
guns no longer had to fire at a range of a few thousand yards
over open sights, as in 1870: they could now be brought into
action from up to five miles, firing from concealed positions;

while recoilless carriages, making it unnecessary to resight the gun after each shot, improved both rate and accuracy of fire. Heavy artillery acquired a range of twenty or more miles—in the case of some exceptional monsters, fifty or sixty—and could crash through all existing fortifications. 1870 had indicated what the Great War of 1914–18 was to confirm—that artillery was to become the central, perhaps the decisive weapon on the battlefield. By 1918 it was artillery that took ground, infantry that held it; and ground derived its importance very largely from the facilities it provided for artillery observation.

What, finally, about cavalry, the oldest, most prestigious arm of all? Its importance for raiding and reconnaissance remained unquestioned—indeed, on the newly-enlarged battlefields, greater than ever before. So also was its mobility in conveying fire-power: the value of 'mounted infantry', the old 'dragoons', was shown very clearly in the wide spaces of South Africa, not to mention the battlefields of the American Civil War. But cavalrymen resisted any suggestion that they would in future be confined to such ancillary rôles, instead of providing that decisive shock in battle which historically they saw as their *raison d'être*. Increased infantry fire power would, they hoped, be neutralized by improved artillery fire power. The greater distances to be covered would not defeat their improved breeds of horses. So 1914 saw all the armies of Europe still equipped with full establishments of cavalry armed with lances and sabres, trained to charge on the battlefield and exploit a breakthrough. In the great spaces of eastern Europe where no continuous fronts were established, cavalry remained effective well into the twentieth century. In western Europe a few weeks were enough to make it clear, to all except some of their own commanders, that heavy cavalry was now an expensive anachronism. Even its rôle in reconnaissance was soon to be taken over by the motor-cycle and the armoured-car.

Military thinkers in general did not underestimate the problems raised by the new weapons. The experiences of 1870 were to be reinforced by those of the Russo-Turkish War of 1877–8, the British-Boer War in South Africa in 1899–1901, and the Russo-Japanese War of 1904–5; all of which illustrated with increasing clarity the capacity of infantry dug into well-prepared positions and armed with modern weapons to inflict unsupportable casualties on assaulting forces. One independent observer, the Polish banker Ivan Bloch, on the basis of careful analysis of weapon performance, concluded in his book *La Guerre Future* (1898) that since it was now statistically impossible for attacks to succeed, war was no longer a viable instrument of policy at all. Military leaders understandably did not draw the same conclusion, but they did not deny that any force launching a frontal attack against prepared positions had to be prepared for very heavy casualties indeed; while outflanking manoeuvres of the kind practised by the German armies in 1870 would call for enormous numbers. In either case the army with the greatest resources in man-power would enjoy a decisive advantage, and between 1871 and 1914 General Staffs vied with one another in demanding ever larger forces as the solution to their problems.

The men who did so with the greatest urgency were the military planners in Berlin. The German General Staff had to plan to fight a two-front war, against both France and Russia. Their problems grew year by year as the development of the railway system in the Russian Empire after 1890 made it possible for the Russian Army to deploy more of its manpower in Europe. When Bismarck's policy of isolating France by remaining on good terms with both the Russian and the Austro-Hungarian Empires was abandoned by his successors, and France and Russia established their entente in 1891, the German General Staff regarded war as only a matter of time. Their problem was on which front to concentrate their forces first. A decisive victory on the pattern of Sedan seemed possible only in the restricted spaces of western Europe; but the French frontier was now so strongly fortified that any such decision there appeared out of the question. The solution proposed by the Chief of the German General Staff, Count Alfred von Schlieffen, is well-known: a wide outflanking movement through Belgium to take the French in the rear, trap them against their own defences and destroy them in a *Schlacht ohne Morgen* which would enable the bulk of the German Army to be transferred eastward to deal with the vaster but more slowly moving threat of the Russian armies. Schlieffen bequeathed this concept to his successors on his retirement in 1905, but the more they examined it the more difficult it appeared to execute. The logistical problems, though enormous, were not insoluble. The fundamental difficulty was to find adequate manpower, and it was necessary in 1912 to pass a new Army Law to increase the size of the German forces yet further.

The French naturally responded in kind, by extending the period which their conscripts had to serve with the colours. But the French General Staff were less concerned than were the Germans over the strength of the defensive in modern war. In the first place they attributed their defeat in 1870 very largely to the passivity with which French generals had defended their positions instead of seizing the initiative in true Napoleonic style and manoeuvring boldly in the presence of the enemy. In the second, as we have already seen, the traditions of the French Army even in the eighteenth century were those of the offensive, and there was little inclination on the part of its commanders to sit behind their defences and allow their adversaries to exhaust themselves in the attack. Ever mindful of the Napoleonic dictum that in war the moral is to the physical as three to one, French military leaders, General Ferdinand Foch foremost among them, continued to believe that even the strongest defences could be carried by mass attacks under heroic leadership, so long as the offensive could build up a decisive superiority of fire. So they planned in 1914 to disrupt the German movements by taking the initiative with their own attacks—attacks in which bloody casualties were to be expected, but from which no strong-willed commander would shrink.

Long before 1914, then, it was accepted by all the states of Europe that the military effectiveness on which they relied to preserve their relative power and status depended, not on the efficiency of small professional forces, but on a combination of the manpower of the population and a strategically appropriate railway network. Any nation that gained a decisive advantage in these two respects, other things being equal, could transform the political map of Europe almost overnight.

The availability and the welfare of that manpower therefore became a matter of state concern as never before. The birth rate itself was an index of military power, and the French watched the decline of theirs after 1870, compared with the soaring figures of their German rivals, with deep concern. The physical health of the conscripts was important: social policy in the United Kingdom owed a great deal to the experience of the 1850s, when it was discovered that an alarmingly high proportion of militiamen called to the colours for the war against Russia had to be rejected as unfit for service. So also were basic educational standards. Modern armies had become complex organizations demanding literacy and numeracy down to a very low level of the hierarchy; a cynic might suggest that it was even more necessary for NCOs to be literate than it was for officers. The common saying that it was the Prussian schoolmasters who won the Franco-Prussian War implied something very different from the comment attributed to Wellington, that the battle of Waterloo was won on the playing fields of Eton.

Not that the traditional qualities of the aristocracy—courage, initiative, independence, leadership—were not equally necessary on battlefields so large that senior officers could only state their intentions in the most general terms and leave it to their juniors to translate them into practice as well as circumstances permitted. It was necessary to have very large quantities of very good officers. These could not be provided from the ranks of the aristocracy alone, even though the slump in land values in the latter part of the century made the landed classes look to the military profession with renewed interest as a source of economic salvation. And even if the aristocracy could still provide the kind of charismatic leadership which was their traditional *raison d'être*, other qualities were increasingly demanded of professional soldiers—an understanding of technology and first-rate administrative ability not least among them. A new kind of professionalism began to develop among regular officers: without ceasing to be heroic leaders they had to learn, in addition, to be managers and engineers.

This change of style was accomplished without too much difficulty in France, where the officer corps had been ever since the Revolution a largely middle-class institution. In the Habsburg Empire the aristocracy had always been flexible and eclectic. In Russia there was never any question of the nobility finding enough officers for the army, which was very largely led by the middle- and lower-middle-class products of cadet training schools known as *junkers*. But in Germany the situation was far less flexible. There, as we have seen, the officer-corps and the monarchy stood in a peculiarly intimate relationship of reciprocal loyalty: the officers swore allegiance to their War Lord and expected confirmation of their privileges in return. As the century entered its troubled middle years, the Prussian officer corps saw itself as the defenders not only of the monarchy against its external adversaries but of the social order against internal forces of disruption. Although they recognized the military necessity for the expansion of the army pressed on them by the General Staff, their leaders viewed with apprehension a process which threatened to swamp their officers' messes with middle-class parvenus from liberal backgrounds, and to fill the ranks with young men infected by socialistic ideas.

They need not have worried. The middle-class radicals of the 1820s and 30s who carried on the intellectual and political ferment of the *Erhebungszeit* were certainly revolutionary in 1848, and continued to constitute a troublesome opposition in the 1850s. But Bismarck drew their sting by persuading the Prussian monarchy to espouse the cause of German nationalism and in 1871 they shouted *Hoch der Kaiser*! as loudly as anyone. Thereafter the German bourgeoisie supported and identified themselves with the Prussian military establishment, were delighted if they could wangle for themselves a commission in the officers' reserve, and were as frightened as anyone by the growth of socialism among the industrialist proletariat. This was particularly alarming to the military authorities. The workers in the big new industrial cities in the Ruhr and the Rhineland had no tradition of loyalty to a feudal master as had the good peasants of Brandenburg and Prussia where the nobility still owned most of the estates. But it was in these cities that population was growing fastest and from which the increment of military manpower had to be recruited; and how reliable would that manpower be—not necessarily against the

French, but against their own brothers, if they were called upon to defend the social order against the revolution which the German upper classes increasingly dreaded?

What the Prussian officer corps feared, Karl Marx and Friedrich Engels hoped. Both were enthusiastic students and shrewd commentators on military affairs: the writings of Engels, in particular, make him one of the foremost military critics of the nineteenth century, displaying as they do both a detailed grasp of military technicalities and profound under-standing of the underlying connections between military developments and social change. Neither had any sympathy for 'bourgeois pacifism'—the ideas inherited by British and French liberals from the Enlightenment, but which in Britain went back to still older roots in the non-conformist churches and were to achieve considerable political significance when expressed by such leaders as Richard Cobden and John Bright. Nor did they hold with the romantic revolutionaries of the 1830s, who believed that insurrections sparked off by élites could overthrow the established order of society. Marx and Engels believed that force always had been an instrument of change in human affairs and always would be, but that such change could take place only in accordance with certain objective laws. A revolutionary situation took time to develop. But the replacement of professional soldiers—a hitherto infallible instrument of repression in the hands of the old order—by armies in which the masses themselves would be trained in the use of firearms and military tactics, was the best augury for the Revolution that could be wished.

What Marx and Engels hoped for and the Prussian officer-corps feared did not come to pass—not, at least, until the Russian Revolution of 1917, when the structure of Russian society had been subjected to a literally intolerable strain. The army of Germany did not become subverted: rather, universal military service, in Germany and elsewhere, proved an efficient instrument of militarization.

'Militarism', like 'Fascism' has become a term of such general illiterate abuse that the scholar must use it with care. Here we mean by it simply an acceptance of the values of the military subculture as the dominant values of society: a stress on hierarchy and subordination in organization, on physical courage and self-sacrifice in personal behaviour, on the need for heroic leadership in situations of extreme stress; all based on an acceptance of the inevitability of armed conflict within the states-system and the consequent need to develop the qualities necessary to conduct it. By the end of the nineteenth century European society was militarized to a very remarkable degree. War was no longer considered a matter for a feudal ruling class or a small group of professionals, but one for the people as a whole. The armed forces were regarded, not as part of the royal household, but as the embodiment of the Nation. Dynastic sovereigns emphasized their rôle as national leaders by appearing whenever possible in uniform; and military parades, military bands, military ceremonial provided an image of the Nation with which all classes could identify themselves.

For militaristic nationalism was not a purely bourgeois phenomenon. When Marx wrote that the working man had no country, he may have spoken truly about the workers of the early industrial revolution, uprooted from a stable social order in the countryside, huddled in wretched conditions in cities which had as yet developed no sense of identity, truly alienated from the society which exploited them. But fifty years later state education, legitimized and powerful trades unions, and, perhaps most important of all, a cheap and lurid press had transformed the situation. By the beginning of the twentieth century the working classes were responding at least as readily to the stimuli of nationalism as they were to those of socialism, and the most successful political leaders were those who could blend the appeals of both. The appeals for class unity across international frontiers were scattered to the winds once the bugles began to blow in 1914.

To suggest, as have some historians, that the frenetic and militaristic nationalism of the early twentieth century was caused by a reactionary ruling class successfully indoctrinating the masses in order to wean their support away from revolution and attract them to the established order is crudely mechanistic. It was in fact the most reactionary elements in the ruling class which mistrusted nationalism the most. The ideas of Hegel and Mazzini had a value and an appeal of their own, and democracy and nationalism fed one another. The greater the sense of participation in the affairs of the State, the more was the State seen as the embodiment of these unique and higher value systems which called it into being, and the greater became the commitment to protect and serve it. Moreover, the Nation appeared as a focus of popular loyalty at a time when the power of organized religion was ebbing. It provided purpose, colour, excitement, and dignity to peoples who had outgrown the age of miracles and had not yet entered that of pop stars. But the Nation could only measure its worth and power against other Nations. However peaceful its purposes and lofty its ideals it became increasingly difficult to avoid the conclusion—and a growing number of thinkers at the turn of the century were making no attempt to avoid it—that its highest destiny was War.

This does something to explain the most remarkable phenomena of 1914—the excited crowds filling the boulevards of every major European city, the British volunteers flocking to the recruiting booths so as to get to France before the fun was over, the French St. Cyriens marching into battle in their passing-out uniforms complete with white gloves and pompoms, the German reservists, university students the previous summer, going singing with linked arms to meet their deaths at the hands of British machine-gunners at Langemarck, the sense almost of ecstasy which emanates from the literature of that time. 1914, like 1789, though it was seen by some as a catastrophic breakdown of a system, perhaps of a civilization, was for others a moment of fulfilment and escape. As in 1789 immense, frustrated energies were released. The masses of men required by military professionals came forward with superabundant goodwill. They marched their boots off to achieve Schlieffen's impossible targets. They threw their lives away without a word of complaint in fulfilment of Joffre's offensive strategy. And they continued to come forward. The enthusiasm which sustained the mass armies of Europe through 1914 began to ebb only two years later; and even then, so far as at least Britain and Germany were concerned, it only settled down into a dour and dogged endurance.

This enthusiasm prevailed, not only in the armies but

throughout the societies that produced them, both reflected in and stoked up by the popular press. Again, it would be a crudely mechanistic and distorted explanation to attribute this simply to propaganda and manipulation by ruling élites: in Britain and France the traditional statesmen, the Asquiths and the Vivianis, who held power in the early part of the war were rudely shouldered aside by more demotic figures, the Lloyd Georges and the Clemenceaus, who could respond more readily to the mood of what we would now call the Radical Right; and even in Germany, where the fall of the civilian Chancellor Bethmann-Hollweg was engineered in 1917 by the High Command, the subsequent military dictatorship of Hindenberg and Ludendorff was supported by a powerful organization, the Fatherland Front, which represented all strata of society but probably drew the bulk of its support from the lower middle classes.

All this made possible something which only a very few clear-sighted prophets had foreseen might be necessary and even fewer had believed would be possible: the total mobilization of all the resources of society for a prolonged struggle lasting for years. Pre-war thinkers had believed that twentieth-century war would be short and decisive because they could not conceive how mass warfare could possibly be anything else. With all men of military age in uniform, who would till the fields and man the factories? Compelled to find the vast sums of money needed to carry on the war, would not the whole machinery of finance collapse—and would it not collapse anyhow once the international framework within which the world system of trade and finance now operated had been torn apart by war? So the war *had* to be over by Christmas, and nobody made any plans what to do if it were not.

But it was not. Not only did the Western Front settle down into stalemate, but the spectacular war of movement on the Eastern Front produced no decisive results. Eighteenth-century statesmen, responsible to no one but their princes, might after so inconclusive and expensive a campaign as that of 1914 have got together at the beginning of 1915 and worked out a satisfactory peace settlement; but the forces of popular enthusiasm, popular expectation, and popular indignation

which had been unleashed in 1914 could be no more easily
reined in again than they had been in 1792. The peoples of
Europe had not sprung to arms and endured, already, terrible
sacrifices in order simply to carry out a minor readjustment of
the balance of power. The Russians, through their newly
established representative institutions, demanded not only
guarantees for their Slav clients in south-eastern Europe that
amounted to the break-up of the Habsburg Empire, but also
that historic goal of Russian foreign policy, Constantinople.
The Germans, with the exception only of a courageous
minority of socialists, demanded territorial acquisitions which
would make them for ever safe against any conceivable
combination of enemies; and the British pledged themselves, in the words of Mr. Asquith, not to sheathe the sword
until the menace of 'Prussian militarism' had been finally
destroyed—until in fact Germany's military defeat was so
total that her political system could be remoulded by her
enemies.

So the war had to go on. In 1915 the belligerents once again
attempted to gain decisions in the field—the Germans in the
east by deep penetrations and outflanking manoeuvres, the
French in the west by a continuation of their frontal attacks,
the British attempting to exploit their maritime power by an
amphibious flanking attack on the Dardanelles. By the end of
that year it was clear that the Napoleonic principles on which
soldiers had been raised for a hundred years—*Niederwer-
fungstrategie*, as the Germans termed it, the strategy of overthrow—were no longer valid. More relevant were those wars
of the seventeenth and eighteenth centuries when the object of
strategy was not the destruction of the enemy army but the
exhaustion of the enemy's economic resources—attrition, or
Ermattungsstrategie. But whereas in the eighteenth century this
was best done by the avoidance of battle, in the twentieth it
was achieved by provoking it: by attacking, without necessarily expecting any major tactical success, in order to compel
the enemy to use up his resources faster than one did oneself.
Such was the reasoning behind the German assault on Verdun
in 1916, and the justification for the prolonging, if not the
initiation, of the British attacks on the Western Front in 1916

and 1917. As one British general put it bluntly, the side with the longest purse would win.

Armies were thus no longer the proxies or champions of nations at war. They were instruments through which the belligerents could bleed one another dry of resources and of men. At the same time that other traditional weapon, the naval blockade, had become grimmer in its purpose. Very quickly the major maritime belligerents, Britain and Germany, abandoned restrictions worked out during three hundred years of naval warfare, reconfirmed as recently as the London Convention of 1909, which confined blockade strictly to those resources which enabled belligerents to make war. Or rather, they worked on the assumption that *all* resources could be, and were, now devoted to the purposes of war. Britain and Germany settled down to impose on one another a reciprocal state of siege. When peace came it was the result not so much of victories in the field as of economic and psychological exhaustion.

The burdens which this kind of warfare imposed on the civilian population were accepted without complaint. Immense war loans were raised. Women took the place of men in the factories and the fields. Civilians forfeited luxuries, submitted to increasingly severe rationing of necessities, tightened their belts as consumer goods disappeared from the shops. In the process fundamental changes took place in the belligerent societies themselves. Governments acquired control over new areas of social and economic life. Pressure for wider participation in government increased and had very largely to be accepted. Trades unions had to be accepted as partners with governments and exacted a price—much as the aristocracy had two centuries earlier—in terms of recognition of privileges and status within society. War taxation levelled out the major inequalities of wealth inherent in the old order. If indeed the militarization of society was the deliberate contrivance of the old élites they made a very bad bargain, for it was to be the patriotic peoples of Europe, sacrificing everything in the search for impossible victories, which were to destroy them. Between 1914 and 1918 the dynastic states of Europe, whose ruling families and dominant aristocracies had survived for five hundred years, were swept into limbo in half as many weeks.

But the professional military who served these dynasties were not swept away. In some states indeed they assumed political power. In others they placed their expertise at the disposal of the successor régimes. And all of them, once peace came, turned their attention to solving the problem, how wars in the future (if their political masters saw fit once more to resort to them) could be fought more skilfully; less wastefully; above all, more decisively.

7

The Wars of the Technologists

One may wonder how it came about that, twenty years after fighting the greatest war in their history, one in which they lost collectively some thirteen million dead, the nations of Europe in 1939 became involved in another conflict; one which was to inflict on their society a yet greater level of destruction and bring their pre-eminence in the world decisively to an end. How did it happen that this was the ironic consequence of what the victorious allies had determined should be a war to end wars?

To answer this question we must get the First World War into proportion. In the last chapter we described how in the nineteenth century developments in weapons technology increased both the destructiveness of war and the demands which it made on the manpower of the nations conducting it. But to counterbalance this grim picture, we should notice also how improvements in transportation and medical science during the same period alleviated at least some of the horrors which had attended war in the pre-industrial age. Before 1870 deaths from sickness in armies normally surpassed death from enemy action by a factor of about five to one. By 1918 this proportion had been reversed. Similarly, before 1815 by far the greater number of those wounded in action either died of their wounds within a few days or were at best incapacitated for life. Thereafter the proportion of the wounded who totally recovered rapidly increased; which makes it necessary to scrutinize the gruesome 'casualty lists' of the First World War with great care in order to distinguish between those killed outright or dying of their wounds, and the large numbers of lightly wounded who returned to duty and may have figured several times on casualty lists without being any the worse.

Improvements in transport ensured also that no troops—at least in western Europe—were subjected to extreme hardship for more than at the very most a few weeks at a time, and that arrangements could be made for their rest and recreation. Finally, with certain horrible exceptions, the citizen soldiers carried over into military life standards of humanity in their treatment both of civilians on the battlefield and of the enemy. Since the wars of the mid-nineteenth century valiant attempts had been made to lay down ground-rules which would make the conduct of war more humane. The International Red Cross Society had been founded after the Franco-Austrian War of 1859. International conferences had met, at Geneva in 1864 and 1906 and the Hague in 1899 and 1907, to regulate the treatment of civilians, of the wounded, and prisoners of war and (with considerably less success) the lethality of the weapons used. Partly as a result of these humanitarian activities and of the continuing operation of the spirit they expressed, the onset of 'mass-war' did not involve a relapse into barbarism. The Red Cross was on the whole respected. Enemy wounded were treated with humanity. Reciprocal caution and international inspection ensured the fair treatment of prisoners of war.

As a result soldiers even in the front areas often lived in conditions which their predecessors would have had good reason to envy. They were regularly and adequately fed. Many of them indeed were better cared for, thanks to the development of ancillary military services, than they had been in civilian life at home. The image of the Great War which later developed in Europe as a period of almost unrelieved horror was not shared by many of the soldiers themselves when they returned to a post-war world which was for many of them disappointing and drab and for some one of real deprivation. At post-war regimental reunions they were able to persuade themselves—perhaps with increasing facility as they grew older—that the war with its comradeship and its adventures, its challenges and triumphs, its economic security and freedom from domestic responsibilities, had really been the happiest time in their lives.[1] This nostalgia for a lost world of security, status, and purpose was to be a significant element in the confused political movements which were in the 1920s to give birth to various forms of Fascism.

For although the experience of the Great War did produce in many countries a deep and widespread reaction against the militarism of the pre-war years, this reaction was by no means universal. There were many who, emerging from an apparently stable world of national loyalties and traditional values into one of chaos, defeat, and revolution, felt themselves betrayed; who sought for scapegoats; who tried to recreate the glamour and security of military hierarchies within new populist organizations; and who saw in the use of violence the path to power both in domestic and international politics. For these movements of the Radical Right, which acquired from their Italian exemplar the generic name of 'Fascism', war was not only a viable instrument of national policy but an activity in which mankind justified itself. So far from reacting against the militaristic nationalism which had been endemic in Europe before the war, they took it to a yet higher pitch of intensity.

But whereas pre-war nationalism had been quite compatible with the ideals of the French Revolution, of Liberty, Equality, and Fraternity, and nations had commanded the loyalties of their citizens largely in the name of those ideals, Fascism set itself up in frank opposition to them. It proclaimed the virtues, not of liberty, but of leadership and submission; not of equality, but of dominance and obedience; not of fraternity, but of racial supremacy. In so doing it was able to appeal to elements in European society which had found in older systems of authority, temporal and ecclesiastical, a satisfaction for psychological needs of which they were unaware until those systems had been destroyed. The manipulation of these needs in Germany, a society rendered particularly vulnerable by revolution and defeat, brought to power a régime whose impact on the international political system was to be as disruptive as that of Revolutionary France. Not only did it challenge the existing power-balance between the states of Europe: it denied the ideological consensus on which the entire international system was based.

A comparable denial had of course already come from

Russia. There the Revolution of 1917 had brought to power a régime which, based on the doctrines of Karl Marx as modified by Lenin, considered itself in a state of perpetual war with the bourgeois world. But after the initial wars of intervention immediately consequent on the Revolution the Soviet Union settled down into a condition of suspicious co-existence with its neighbours to the west; who in their turn saw in Russia a danger to the internal stability of their régimes, through her manipulation of indigenous communist parties, rather than a serious military threat. The fear which obsessed the ruling classes of Europe between the wars was that of 'Bolshevism' at home rather than of Soviet aggression. It was strong enough to lead many among them to welcome Fascism as an ally against the threat from the Left and to blind them to the far more immediate danger which it posed to internal and international stability.

Post-war Europe thus found itself tugged between three competing ideologies. In appearance 1918 had seen the triumph of nations who adhered to the principles of liberal democracy stemming from the Enlightenment, who proposed to use their victory to establish an international Rule of Law and to renounce war as an instrument of policy; ideas which had germinated and come to fruition during the nineteenth century in the peaceful and prosperous soil of Britain and North America. In practice the Great War, by destroying so much of the traditional framework of European society, had greatly strengthened the revolutionary forces both of the Left, who believed that the millenium would not come without further armed conflict both national and international, and of the Right, who saw in the continuation of international conflict the necessary destiny of man. The victorious powers were therefore in a position to enforce their ideology only if they had the strength to do so, which in the absence of the United States they had not. As a result, fifteen years after the Versailles settlement, the nations of Europe found themselves once again preparing for war.

The kind of war which Fascism glorified was not that fought by masses of hapless conscripts at the behest of generals far behind the lines. It was one which would be conducted by small teams of young heroes, airmen, tank-crews, storm-troops, 'supermen' who by daring and violence would wrest the destiny of mankind from the frock-coated old dodderers round their green baize tables and shape a cleaner, more glorious future. War would, they hoped, in future be a business for élites. They were not altogether wrong. Technology, which in the nineteenth century had made mass participation in warfare both possible and necessary, was in the twentieth to place increasing power in the hands of highly qualified technicians. The Second World War was to see a curious blend of mass participation and deadly esoteric duels between technological experts. By the second half of the century the peoples of Europe were to be extruded almost totally from conflicts which, if they came, would be fought by comparatively small numbers of military technicians wielding destructive power on an almost inconceivable scale.

To understand how this came about we must now retrace our steps and consider certain developments in nineteenth-century warfare with which we did not deal in the last chapter.

Technology in the nineteenth century made it possible to mass-produce weapons which were not only increasingly effective but easy to manipulate. For the infantry, cartridges eliminated the need to manipulate powder and shot; breech-loading eliminated the ram-rod; magazines and bolt action gave a rapidity of fire, and calibrated sights an accuracy, which made of every conscript within a few weeks a marksman with whom the oldest Grenadier in Frederick the Great's Prussian Guard could never have begun to compete. So also with artillery: breech-loading and recoilless carriages eliminated the tedious business of swabbing-out and relaying after each shot which had made the old cannon such a slow and erratic weapon even in the hands of experts. With a few drill movements, some simple calculations read off a table, and a plentiful supply of high explosive shell, a regiment of field guns could in 1914 deliver on to a target area of a few hundred square yards more destructive power in an hour than had been fired by all the guns on both sides in the whole course of the Napoleonic wars. All this could be done by conscripts after a few months' training. Mass production of these weapons made necessary mass production of men.

In a society economically so close-knit as that of Europe, any advantage given by the possession of technically superior weapons was temporary and unlikely in itself to be decisive. Numbers were what mattered. Yet there does come a point when range and destructiveness of fire power is in itself enough to carry the day; when a technically inferior power, even if numerically superior, does not have the chance to show its fighting qualities and it is obvious even before the battle begins what the outcome is going to be.

Such an advantage was enjoyed by the European Powers in their colonial wars in the nineteenth century. We saw in chapter III how at the beginning of the sixteenth century it was their monopoly of guns that enabled the Portuguese to break into and dominate the trading system of the Indian Ocean. But as the use of firearms became general throughout the world the advantage which Europeans gained from them disappeared. In the eighteenth century it was the professional qualities of drill and discipline, together with a careful attention to their supply system, that gave European armies such an ascendancy in, for example, India, rather than the weapons with which they were armed. But in the nineteenth century the balance swung decisively in favour of the technologically superior powers. Their railways opened up the interior of Africa and Asia and gave their armies a mobility which compensated for the smallness of their size; a factor as important in the Russian colonization of central Asia and the American drive to the west as it was for the imperial expansion of the European powers. European artillery, breech-loading rifles, and machine-guns made the outcome of any fighting almost a foregone conclusion.*

* Almost, but not quite. The confident reassurance of Hilaire Belloc's Captain Blood,

> Whatever happens, we have got
> The Gatling gun, and they have not

was not always valid, as the British survivors of the Zulu victory at Isandhlwana in 1879 and the Italian survivors of the Ethiopian victory at Adowa in 1896 would have been able to testify. Even superior weapons, if deployed without tactical skill and used against forces superior in leadership and courage, did not

But there was one area of European conflict where technological development was, during the later part of the nineteenth century, beginning to appear profoundly destabilizing;
where it looked as if it might provide an advantage sufficient
not just to win a battle but to win a war and to establish a new
kind of political dominance. That was naval warfare.

It is difficult not to sympathize with nineteenth-century
naval officers who had within the space of a single generation
to adjust their thinking, their ships, their weapons, and their
tactics from the age of Nelson to that of von Tirpitz, from the
scale of H.M.S. *Victory* to that of the *Dreadnought*, knowing that
if they lagged behind the result might be disastrous for their
country. In the twentieth century their predicament was to
become common to all the Services. Every new technological
development from the steam-engine to nuclear fission had
implications for warfare which had to be scrutinized and
exploited. The military profession had to become increasingly
versatile: at the same time as it was expanding to act as a
cadre for the new mass armies, it had to establish technological
and scientific branches to develop and service the new weapons
systems—branches whose activities were in the twentieth
century to achieve an almost overriding importance. W. S.
Gilbert's picture of a modern Major-General who had all
scientific knowledge at his finger-tips may have made Vic-
torian audiences titter, but there was soon to be little place in
the senior ranks of any armed service for officers who lacked
the intellectual flexibility to keep abreast of technical change
and ensure that their side exploited it first.

The naval competition of the nineteenth century presents a
picture familiar for our own day. As today a successful
exploitation of nuclear physics and missile technology is seen
to give one state a devastating advantage over its neighbour—
so devastating that it could destroy it without having to fight
at all—so in the nineteenth century it began to appear possible
for the nation which most effectively applied in its naval

---

necessarily guarantee victory. Colonial conquest still owed at least as much to the
superior cohesion, organization, and above all self-confidence of the Europeans
as it did to their weapons.

building programmes the developing techniques of marine engineering, metallurgy, and artillery construction to pulverize any opposing fleet without its victim being able to land a single shot on its assailant. Already in the 1840s steam engines gave a decisive advantage in speed and manoeuvrability over sail, especially in narrow waters like the Channel and the Mediterranean where the sea-keeping qualities of sail were of minor importance. It began to look to worried British statesmen as if the ascendancy which Nelson's navy had established over the French in these theatres was a thing of the past. The use of iron in ship construction made it possible to break free from the limitations imposed by wood. Whereas Nelson's ships had been, at most, of 2,000 tons displacement, the iron vessels in the 1860s were of 9,000 tons, and by the end of the century of 20,000 tons. This weight was accounted for not simply by increases in size, but also by the increasing thickness of armour plating, and this in turn was made necessary by the increasing calibre and range of guns which could be mounted as ships increased in size; guns which, because they were too heavy to be mounted to fire broadside, were housed centrally in turrets with a traverse of up to 180°, and developed ranges of up to 20,000 yards.

Progress from the sailing ship of the line to the ironclad man-of-war was marked by chaos in design. The Russians designed an entirely circular ship. One British model which tried to combine iron, steam, *and* a full rig of sail capsized and sank with all hands. And it was marked also by great and understandable nervousness. The Russians had shown at the outset of the Crimean War that ironclads firing shell could destroy an entire fleet of wooden sailing ships, and the famous encounter in 1862 between the two ironclads, the *Merrimac* and the *Monitor*, in Hampton Roads during the American Civil War led British publicists to argue that virtually the whole of the Royal Navy had now to be considered obsolete. So the last half of the nineteenth century saw a frantic competition between the British on the one hand and their chief imperial rivals, the French and the Russians on the other—a competition in size of guns, thickness of armour, and speed. At the very end of the century the Germans joined in the race with all the power of the most highly developed industry in Europe behind them. Within five years of their doing so, at the Battle of Tsushima in 1904 the Japanese, by destroying the entire Russian fleet, gave an alarming illustration of the fate which awaited any navy which allowed itself to become technologically out of date. The real competition was now, not at sea, but in the dockyards; and Germans and British set to to outbuild one another in the new all big-gun ships, *Dreadnoughts* and *Super-Dreadnoughts*, on which command of the sea and with it, so it was thought, command of the world now appeared to depend.

The Battleship was indeed a symbol of national pride and power of a unique kind; one even more appropriate to the industrial age than armies. It embodied at once the technological achievement of the nation as a whole, its world-wide reach and, with its huge guns, immense destructive power. It was a status symbol of universal validity, one which no nation conscious of its destiny could afford to do without.

But paradoxically it was a symbol of a power about whose continued possession all the nations of Europe were becoming increasingly anxious. It was a great relief for the British to know that fifty battleships could be mustered for the Diamond Jubilee review at Spithead in 1897 without denuding any overseas station; yet they knew that they were losing the industrial lead which had enabled them to dominate the world for a hundred years, and they realized how vulnerable they would be should their ships ever lose command of the sea. Admiral von Tirpitz's ships were the perfect embodiment of the achievements and aspirations of the Second German Reich—of the booming middle classes of west Germany rather than the military landlords of the east; but they could not make up for the haunting sense of vulnerability of a people always squeezed between two powerful rivals, an implacable France seeking revenge after 1870 and the enormous potential of the Russian Empire. Battleships could do little to console Frenchmen for their demographic inferiority, nor the Russians for their technological backwardness, nor the Austrians for the threat which nationalism posed to their Empire. And there could be no clearer indication of the change which was coming over the international system than the fact that the last naval war of the nineteenth century and the first of the twentieth saw the defeat of European fleets at the hands of non-European naval powers: Spain at the hands of the United States in 1898, Russia at the hands of Japan in 1904.

When war came in 1914, Britain and her allies were still ahead in the naval race, and Tirpitz's High Seas Fleet could do no more than pin down their adversary in a game of cat and mouse. But German technological ingenuity opened up opportunities in another direction with the development of ocean-going submarines. With these an entirely new chapter in the history of naval warfare began.

It had been the general expectation in 1914 that command of the sea would be settled, as it had been in the days of Nelson, by the clash of great capital fleets. The victor in such an encounter, it was assumed, would then be able to chase the enemy's small craft and commerce raiders from the oceans and impose on his victim a blockade which, for thickly-populated countries dependent upon overseas trade and imported food-stuffs, could only be ruinous. This was the doctrine preached by the American naval historian and theorist, Alfred Thayer Mahan, whose work *The Influence of Sea Power on History* (1890) became the Bible of European navies at the turn of the century. Although the destruction of trade was the ultimate object, taught Mahan, it was fallacious to use naval power, as had the French in the seventeenth and eighteenth centuries, to attack that trade directly. The task of naval power was to gain 'Command of the Sea', which made it possible to use the oceans as a highway for one's own trade and a barrier to that of the enemy; and that command was the perquisite of the strongest capital fleet.

Mahan was vindicated by the events of the Great War in so far as the British Navy was able to impose a blockade of increasing severity on Germany which Tirpitz's High Seas Fleet was too weak to challenge; cutting her off from free communication not only with her colonies, which were unimportant, but with such powerful neutral trading partners as the United States, which were very important indeed—although the process strained relations between Britain and the United States almost to breaking point, as it had a hundred years before. But the development of the submarine, from the short-range weapon for coastal protection as which it was originally conceived, into an ocean-going vessel with a cruising capacity calculable in weeks, enabled Germany to retaliate with terrible effectiveness.

But although submarines could impose a blockade, they could not operate according to principles of Prize Law laid down for the age of sail; forcing a vessel suspected of carrying contraband to heave to, searching her, placing a prize crew on board to take her to the nearest port where a Prize Court could adjudicate on the propriety of impounding her cargo. At best they could search their victim and give its crew time to take to the boats before sinking her. But for a submarine to surface at all was to render itself vulnerable to the smallest armed merchantman. The temptation to sink at sight and ask questions afterwards was overwhelming. The Germans restrained their submarine commanders from considerations of prudence rather than humanity: such isolated instances as the sinking of the *Lusitania* in 1915, which was probably carrying contraband but was certainly carrying a number of American citizens, made it clear that unrestricted submarine warfare would add the United States to the already large number of Germany's enemies. But by the end of 1916 the prospects for the complete defeat of Britain by blockade appeared so promising and those for any decision of the war by land appeared so bleak that the German High Command decided that this was a risk which had to be run. Four months later the United States entered the war.

It was not so much the physical contribution made by the United States forces when they reached Europe in 1918 as the moral reinforcement brought by the prospect of her resources being placed at the disposal of the Allies that decided the outcome of the war. But if the submarine had not been mastered in 1917 there might have been no Allies left for the United States to succour. Victory in anti-submarine warfare required not only the development of such specialized apparatus as depth charges and location devices, but a revolution in British naval thinking; an acceptance that the defensive was a more effective means of destroying submarines than the offensive, that merchant shipping should be convoyed not only for its own protection but to provide a bait, that such light craft as destroyers were better employed on escorting these convoys than on protecting the Grand Fleet. And it involved the perfection of techniques of communication and interception of enemy communications—techniques which the invention of radio were beginning to make virtually a fourth dimension of war.

In naval war, therefore, the participation of the mass of the population was irrelevant. It was a contest between the courage and endurance of the small groups of professional fighting-men manning the vessels themselves, including the aircraft which were soon to be added to the resources of the submarine-hunters; the ingenuity of those even smaller groups of scientists, technologists, and cryptographers responsible for developing their weapons and communications systems; and the rival skill and judgement of the commanders and staffs who planned and conducted the campaign. Expertise in electronics was at least as important as seamanship. Success ultimately went to the side which was able to track the movements of its adversary and read his signals while keeping its own secret, and by the Second World War techniques of radar-scanning and radio-interception had been developed which made this possible. The crews of the submarines and of the surface vessels and aircraft hunting them were the instruments in a deadly game of hide and seek which might decide the entire outcome of the war.

An identical pattern of conflict between small groups of highly trained fighting men manipulating complex weapons-systems, of competing technologists, and of commanders exercising control at very long distance, was to emerge with the development of war in the air.

Air warfare originated during the First World War as an ancillary aspect of the land battle, as aircraft fought each other for freedom to carry out their primary task of reconnaissance. Only very slowly, as aircraft increased in range, speed, and armament, did it become clear that an air force which enjoyed command of the air over the battlefield might act not only as the eyes of the artillery but as a substitute for the artillery, and on a scale which might make all movement on and behind the battlefield impossible. In war at sea recognition of the effectiveness of air power was equally slow to dawn. Aircraft were obviously useful for reconnaissance and for harassing, but that they might have the capacity to sink ships, even battleships, in spite of all the defences that might be deployed against them, was something that naval commanders were understandably reluctant to admit. The inter-war years were loud with the squabbles between air forces who persistently overrated the capacity of their weapons and navies which continued defiantly to underrate them; a situation understandable enough in view of the speed with which technology was developing and the impossibility of effectively replicating in peacetime conditions of active service. It was to take the experiences of the war in the Pacific after 1941 to show conclusively that the aircraft carrier had replaced the battleship as the primary instrument of naval domination.

Understanding of the potentialities of air power in war by sea and by land was perhaps yet further delayed by the reluctance of air force leaders themselves to address their full attention to the problem. The early enthusiasts for air power were concerned to show not so much that air forces would change the nature of war by sea and land as that they would make it unnecessary. The outcome of the Great War, they maintained, had made it clear that war was no longer decided by traditional military skills. It had shown that armies in the field could not be defeated so long as they could be kept supplied with manpower and munitions. War in the twentieth century was not, as it had been in the past, a conflict between armed forces alone, or even between treasuries. It was one between the will-power and the *morale* of the belligerent populations. What had ultimately brought the war to an end had been, not military victory in itself, but the disintegration of what had now become known as 'the Home Front': the solidarity of the civilian population behind its leaders, their willingness to go on bearing the burdens of deprivation and suffering which 'the war effort' demanded. Peace, they argued, had come as the result of revolution or fear of revolution, not through victory in the field.

If then the centre of gravity of the war effort was not the armies, but the civil populations, and if the object of fighting was now to impose an unendurable burden on the enemy population by wearing out its armies, would it not be more effective to attack that centre of gravity directly, rather than by a process of attrition from which the conquerors themselves emerged almost as exhausted and bankrupt as the conquered? And would not the total of suffering, calculated as it would be in days and weeks rather than in years, be infinitely less? Above all, would not the fear of receiving such blows, against which there could be no possible defence, be the greatest possible *deterrent* against any power which contemplated a breach of the peace?

This was the argument of, among others, the Italian Colonel Giulio Douhet, whose book *Command of the Air* enjoyed a wide circulation in the 1920s. It was also the argument of the founding fathers of the British Royal Air Force, in particular Air Chief Marshal Sir Hugh Trenchard, who used it to justify the creation of a Service with a strategic rôle entirely independent of the surface forces. Continental airmen found greater difficulty in resisting the institutional pressures which subordinated them to the powerful armies on whose achievements national security traditionally depended; but in Britain the expansion during the Great War of the small Imperial gendarmerie which served as a peacetime army into a force capable of intervention on a continental scale was regarded (not least by the soldiers themselves) as an atypical and disagreeable experience under no circumstances to be repeated. So when in the 1930s Britain began with enormous reluctance to re-arm, resources were allocated, not to an army equipped to fight a traditional land campaign, but to an air force capable of striking terror into the heart of the enemy—a capacity which would, it was hoped, deter Germany from initiating war at all.

As it happened, the British aircraft industry showed itself unable to compete with the German, and it was Germany who first built up an air force apparently capable of inflicting immediate and unavoidable destruction on her neighbour's cities; a threat which Hitler used to good effect in the implementation of his policy. It was taken for granted that there could be no defence against air attack—that the bomber, in the words of Stanley Baldwin, would always get through. It was also assumed, largely on the basis of two German air raids on London in July 1917, that the bomber, having got through, would wreak havoc on a vast and unacceptable scale. Events were to show both assumptions to be, if not false, at least greatly over-stated. In the later 1930s the development of fast-climbing low-wing monoplanes, and of radar interception techniques to give early warning of enemy attack, made it possible for defending forces to exact an unacceptably high price from bombers attempting to penetrate deep into their territory by day. When attacking forces took to bombing by night it took them some time to learn how to use radar offensively by the projection of beams which made possible accurate blind navigation, and scanning devices which revealed the topography of the ground through darkness or cloud. Even then the defence developed night-fighters and learned how to confuse the electronic directional signals on which the attack depended. Like war at sea, war in the air became an immensely sophisticated exercise in tactical and technical ingenuity in which the professional fighting men were at least as dependent on the expertise of the scientist as they were on their own skills to carry out their task. It was only in the last years of the war, after a struggle demanding the full participation of the United States as well as the Royal Air Force, that the Allies secured a command of the air over Germany sufficient to enable them to inflict the degree of destruction on the enemy homeland that the prophets of air power had foretold. And even then civilian morale remained intact. The German people went stoically on with their business and obeyed their government until the very end of the war.

The impact of technological change on the conduct of war by land was more diffuse. Within a few months of the outbreak of war in 1914 it had been realized that the internal combustion engine might be used to drive fighting vehicles as well as

transportation. Within two years the first 'tanks' were in action.
But the design and use of these early armoured fighting
vehicles was geared to the requirements of trench warfare.
They were seen primarily as mobile fire power to help the
attack break into the enemy's defensive lines; and once the
first tactical surprise was over it was not too difficult to find
means of countering them. The most spectacular breakthrough
of the war, that achieved by the Germans on the Western
Front in March 1918, was not the work of tanks at all, but of
infantry. The Germans deployed, not in long lines of riflemen
as had always been habitual, but as small groups of 'storm
troops' armed with mortars, light machine-guns, and grenades,
by-passing strong-points and penetrating wherever they found
weakness, operating with an independence and flexibility such
as had hardly been seen in Europe since the skirmishes in the
early campaigns of the French Revolution. But the value both
of armoured fighting vehicles and of these storm units was
limited once they outran their communications and their
artillery cover; the first dependent on highly vulnerable
field-telephone lines, the second on field guns which had to be
moved up over a devastated battlefield and re-ranged for new
targets.

It was practical problems such as these that made armies
between the wars reluctant to adopt the more ambitious ideas
of such prophets of armoured warfare as J. F. C. Fuller and
B. H. Liddell Hart in England, Charles de Gaulle in France,
Heinrich Guderian in Germany, and Marshal Tukhachevski
in the Soviet Union. The pictures which these thinkers painted
of entire divisions composed of tanks breaking through enemy
defences, and surging through the gaps in an 'expanding
torrent' to overwhelm the nerve centres in the rear were
exhilarating, but they left a large number of questions un-
answered. How were these units to keep in touch with their
rear? How were they to be kept supplied? What about their
heavy fire support? Why should they not be surrounded and
cut off? If tanks could make a breach in a front, could not
tanks used in a counter-attack just as effectively seal it?
Technological development helped to solve some of these
problems: but for the development of radio communications,

for example, such mobile warfare would have been out of the question. But so sceptical was the High Command even of the German Army that it needed the personal intervention of Hitler to initiate the development of the first Panzer Divisions in 1934, and even the effectiveness of such divisions was discounted as late as 1938 not only by the High Command of the French Army but by one of the founding fathers of armoured warfare, the British specialist B. H. Liddell Hart, who was already devising means of countering them by a combination of minefields, anti-tank guns, and armoured counter-attack.

Certainly the *blitzkrieg* tactics of 1940 and 1941 need not have worked so effectively as they did. In their attack on the West in May 1940 the Germans took very great risks—risks indeed so great that the strategic concept behind their attack had at first been dismissed out of hand by the German High Command and it required, again, Hitler's intervention to make them accept it. Competent adversaries who kept their heads might have sealed off the penetration achieved by the German armoured spearheads in the Ardennes, and the campaign would have gone down to history as a disastrous gamble. Like Napoleon's victories it owed its success primarily to the demoralization of opponents who, after the leisurely pace of previous conflicts, could not adjust themselves to tactics based so overwhelmingly on speed, concentration, and surprise. And in 1941 against Soviet forces already disorganized by the massive political *épuration* of their officer corps three years earlier, the success was to be even more far-reaching.

But such tactics could be rapid and decisive only against unprepared adversaries. The sceptics were in the long run right. If tanks could attack, tanks could counter-attack. An environment could be treated with mines and anti-tank weapons in which armour could barely operate at all; and in any case its successful operation depended largely on maintaining command of the air over the battlefield as well. Armour could achieve little except in close co-operation with highly-trained infantry capable of moving at speed, and artillery also had to be put on tracks in order to keep up. All this demanded

THE WARS OF THE TECHNOLOGISTS

hundreds of vehicles whose requirements in terms of supplies, petrol, and ammunition made necessary the co-operation of thousands more. The interwar dream of small, swift, skilful units operating against each others' supply lines, securing maximum decisions with minimum of cost, turned into the reality of huge armies with massive 'tails', highly vulnerable to enemy air attack and demanding considerable logistical ingenuity to keep them moving at all.

So armies in the Second World War, as in the First, depended heavily on conscript manpower for their effectiveness; not so much because of their size as because of their complexity. The armies of 1914–18 consisted basically of great numbers of infantry armed with a limited range of standard weapons, whose logistical needs could be met very largely by railways and a simple shuttle service between the railheads and what was in most cases a fairly stable front line. In the Second World War fighting units were highly diversified. The inventory of the simple infantry battalion contained not only rifles and grenades but two types of mortar, two kinds of machine-gun, light tracked vehicles, anti-tank guns, hand-held anti-tank weapons, and several types of mine. The demands of armoured units were many times more complex; those of amphibious and airborne units more complex still. So a far greater proportion of the manpower in at any rate Western armies was absorbed in servicing and supplying fighting units than in manning them: in repairing and maintaining vehicles, weapons, and communications systems, in driving supply vehicles, manning depots and hospitals, and ensuring that the whole drab mass was administered, fed and paid.* If in land warfare there was not the same total dependence on scientists working at the frontiers of knowledge to obtain a vital technological advantage as there was at sea and in the air, armies were none the less dependent on technical efficiency at every level and in all branches to be able to function at all. The best fighting soldier found himself helpless

---

* In the Soviet Union the proportion of 'teeth' to 'tail' was considerably higher: the bulk of infantry units operated on scales and with weapons comparable to those of the Western front in the Great War, and depended almost wholly on horse-borne transport. Only their armoured and élite infantry divisions approached the technological sophistication common in the West.

if his radio communications failed and his transport broke down; and the most successful generals tended to be those whose radio-interception services were able to bring them the promptest and most accurate information about the intentions of their opponents.

So a very large proportion of the men and women called up into the armed forces found themselves employed in the same activities—as motor-mechanics, radio-operators, waitresses, or cooks—as in peacetime. Those who were not called up were left alone largely because they were considered to be contributing more to the war effort in their civilian capacity as miners, agricultural workers, lathe operators, or civil servants than they could in uniform. The traditional distinction between soldier and civilian, which had been so clear in the eighteenth and nineteenth centuries and which had even survived the First World War, once again disappeared; particularly since air warfare put civilians at just as great risk as all but a small proportion of the men in the armed forces. One was likely to be a great deal safer as a storeman in an ordnance depot or a waiter in an officers' mess in a military base than as a dock worker or a shop assistant in Liverpool or Hamburg.

So although the era of mass armies supported by the fanatical nationalism of the civil population had passed, the Second World War was, in a far more profound sense, a conflict between entire societies almost as absolute as those of the Dark Ages: a struggle in which every individual felt his value system as well as his physical survival to be threatened by alien forces with which there could be neither communication nor compromise. This was to be seen at its most absolute on the Eastern Front, where the objectives of the leaders of the Third Reich were those of their forefathers a thousand years earlier—the settlement of new territories and the extermination or enslavement of the native populations. It was the capacity of the Soviet government to mobilize every scrap of the huge resources of the Soviet peoples, moral and material, for a struggle to the death against the invader which turned the scale, rather than any techniques of generalship or miracles of technology. Like Napoleon, the Germans relied on the sheer impetus of their attack to secure a decisive victory, and when it failed they lacked the resources to sustain a prolonged struggle against adversaries on the scale of the Soviet Union and the United States.

Nevertheless technology had introduced a factor which had not been present in the Napoleonic era, and which rendered all comparisons with the past of very doubtful value. A little more concentration by the Germans on the development of jet aircraft might have changed the course of the air war. Had they devoted more resources to missile technology they might have produced rocket weapons which would have laid central London waste and made the Allied landings in Normandy impossible. And if their nuclear research had taken a rather different turn and received greater political backing, they might have developed nuclear weapons, in the face of which the heroism of the Soviet peoples and the massive armadas of the Western allies would have been as ineffective as the charges of the Mahdi's tribesmen against Kitchener's armies at Omdurman.

As it was, the first two atomic bombs were dropped on Japan by the United States in August 1945, each destroying a fair-sized city, between them killing 130,000 people outright. Used by one extra-European power against another, in termination of a conflict between them in which Europeans had figured only as auxiliaries, they marked the end of that era of European world dominance which the voyages of Columbus and Vasco da Gama had opened nearly five hundred years earlier. And they marked the close of the age of mass-warfare, of conflicts in which the fully-mobilized populations of industrialized countries had devoted their full energies to overthrowing one another. Within a few years thermonuclear weapons were to be developed, each containing more destructive power than had been used by mankind in its entire recorded history, with missiles capable of delivering them within minutes to any point on the surface of the world. Was there to be any place in the nuclear age for the traditional skills of professional soldiers or for the loyal participation of patriotic peoples? Had 'war', as it had been understood and conducted in Europe for a thousand years, come to an end?

The Nuclear Age

It would be premature even to attempt to answer the questions posed at the end of the last chapter. Only thirty years have passed since the end of the Second World War. Forty years elapsed after the Napoleonic Wars before any of the great powers of Europe engaged in even limited conflict with one another; nearly a hundred before there was another great war involving them all. Certainly there was in 1945 little of the expectation so characteristic of 1918, that the war to end wars had been fought and that a new, happier era had dawned in the history of mankind. Once the brief euphoria of victory had cleared, the ideological hostility between the Soviet Union and the world of liberal capitalism reappeared as irreconcilable as ever. Within a few months misunderstandings had led to non-cooperation; within a few years non-cooperation led to military confrontation and a level of armaments unprecedented in peace time. By the 1950s the international order appeared to rest on nothing more substantial than what a leading American strategic analyst, Albert Wohlstetter, termed 'a delicate balance of terror'.

The passage of time has made it possible to suggest, cautiously, that in fact peace rests on a rather less precarious basis: the acceptance by the major world powers of the *status quo* as the only feasible framework for the conduct of their policies, and a common reluctance to tolerate any major disturbance; the basis, in fact, on which the peace of Europe rested for half a century after the Napoleonic wars. But to maintain political stability indefinitely in a period of economic and social change so rapid as that we have witnessed since 1945 calls for gifts of wisdom in formulating policy and skill in conducting it such as Providence has hitherto doled out with a rather parsimonious hand. But one can at least assert with a reasonable degree of confidence that any future wars fought within the framework of the European system will, for two very good reasons, be of a fundamentally different character from those whose development has been traced in this book.

In the first place 'Europe' as a self-contained system of states, has ceased to exist; much as the Italian system of states ceased to exist when, at the end of the fifteenth century, those powerful auxiliaries invoked by its members to support their quarrels, the House of Habsburg and the House of Valois, moved in to divide the peninsula between them. 'European history' ended within a single week in December 1941, when the first counter-attacks of the Red Army north of Moscow revealed the massive power of the Soviet Union, and the attack at Pearl Harbor brought the United States as a full belligerent into the Second World War. These two states, both deriving their culture from European roots but commanding resources on a scale to dwarf all European powers, were to create new political and economic systems of which they were to be the centres, and whose frontier was to divide Europe down the line of the eastern marches of the Carolingian Empire. In future, as with the former Italian states, any conflict between European states on anything but the most local level would involve the participation of their patrons, and vice versa. A war in Europe would be a local conflict within a confrontation of global dimensions, and could be considered and planned for only within that context.

Secondly Europe had not only ceased to be a self-contained system of states; it had ceased to be the centre of the world political system. Until the fifteenth century the European system had co-existed with many others in the world, communications with most of which were intermittent or non-existent. Then Europe expanded first her geographical knowledge, then her trade, then her military power; until by the end of the nineteenth century a single world political system had been created of which Europe was undisputed head and centre, and very few parts could remain unaffected by European wars. After the Second World War this world pattern disappeared, yielding place to one of whose complexity such terms as 'bi-polarity· or 'multi-polarity' give a totally inadequate descrip-tion. Within this new system the states of Europe were to retain considerable economic importance since their continent remained one of the wealthiest areas in the world, but their political significance was to derive primarily from their position as the most sensitive point of contact between the two 'super-powers'. This very sensitivity was to keep conflict within the area frozen. Wars were to break out almost anywhere except in Europe; but since they occurred mainly in those areas of former European dominance where force had to serve as the midwife at the birth of new states and new régimes, European powers long retained a residual interest in their conduct—if not as participants, then as advisers, trainers, or armourers to the forces involved.

By the last quarter of the twentieth century the forms of international armed conflict were to be almost infinite. Central among them were those 'conventional' conflicts, waged with weapons recognizable as the descendants of those used in the Second World War, although more sophisticated and expen-sive, and becoming increasingly so year by year as research continued into missile technology and electronics. By the 1970s the development of, in particular, precision-guided missiles whose launchers were capable of rapid movement on the battle-field and even portable by infantry, were beginning to cast doubt on two of the most devoutly held beliefs inherited from the Second World War—the dominance over the battlefield of manned aircraft, and the dominance on the battlefield of the heavy battle tank. But general staffs found themselves in the same quandary as they had been a hundred years earlier. They knew that the experience from which they had to extrapolate was out of date; but the only means they had of checking it were from brief conflicts, primarily in the Middle East and the Indian sub-continent, from whose peculiar circumstances it was difficult to draw any very firm conclusions.

It was becoming clear, however, that such weapons—missiles, supersonic aircraft, nuclear-powered submarines, and anti-submarine frigates—were beyond the capacity of all but the most technologically advanced countries to manufacture, the most educated armed forces to operate and maintain, or the wealthiest states to possess in anything but minuscule quantities. The paradoxical situation therefore arose that, thanks to the relative stability of the industralized world, the states best able to manufacture such weapons were those which had least need of them; while those which faced the most serious prospect of armed conflict with their neighbours could afford to possess and operate them on only a very limited scale and were dependent on the wealthy states of the northern hemisphere for their supply. In many new nations indeed the possession of a small quantity of such sophisticated 'hardware' became a status symbol comparable to the minute but immaculate armies maintained by the German princelings of the eighteenth century.

At the most sophisticated end of the scale were nuclear weapons, of which those who possessed them tried with a fair degree of success to preserve a monopoly, but whose possession conferred on their owner a degree of international prestige that made that monopoly increasingly precarious. The Soviet Union caught up with the United States in 1949 in the possession of fission bombs with a yield in the kiloton range. Thereafter the two super-powers raced neck and neck in the development of thermonuclear bombs, of intercontinental missiles, of submarine launchers, of multiple warheads, and the entire apparatus of destruction on a scale so gigantic that it would tax the most fertile imagination to visualize the political circumstances in which it could be appropriately used. The rationale behind this development however was not use, but 'deterrence'; the creation of a state of reciprocal assurance that the initiation of the use of nuclear weapons by one side would lead to instant, inescapable, and unacceptable retaliation by the other.

If the two giants were not to be immobilized within their huge armouries, like millionaires whose wealth could not be converted into acceptable currency, they also needed armed forces more appropriate to their political ambitions and to the problems of the real world. The possession of dependent allies in all parts of the world justified for the United States the continued possession of a navy whose very existence was challenge enough to the Soviet Union to create one to match it. The existence of long, vulnerable land frontiers, east and west, and the need to police her restive European satellites, made it impossible for the Soviet Union to contemplate the disbandment of its great army. But the presence of the Soviet Army on their doorstep created major problems for the states of western Europe. Wealthy and populous though they were, they found it impossible to achieve the degree of political and economic unity which alone would have enabled them to raise armed forces on the same scale as the Soviet Union. After a half-hearted effort to do so at the beginning of the 1950s, they relapsed into dependence on the deterrent effect of American nuclear power.

Within a decade the Soviet Union was in a position not only to overawe western Europe with its conventional forces but to threaten the United States with its own nuclear arsenal, and the defence of western Europe became a more complex matter. Britain and France acquired small nuclear forces of their own, but these possessed no credibility as deterrents to anything save attacks on their own territory. The United States equipped its European allies with 'tactical' nuclear weapons—bombs or missiles sufficiently limited in yield for use in a battlefield rôle; but since even their limited yield was likely to cause civilian casualties in the order of millions the circumstances under which they could be used were never entirely clear. It was probably best that they should be left unclear. The confusion of Western strategic plans was not perhaps so important as it sometimes appeared to worried analysts. The essential need was to provide the assurance that a Soviet attack would be met by immediate and bitter resistance. There might be no certainty that such resistance would immediately or eventually lead to the use of nuclear weapons, but there was equally little certainty that it would not.

In any case, during the decade and a half following the end of the Second World War, the armed forces of the two victorious European powers, Britain and France, had more immediate problems on their hands in attempting to police Empires whose disintegration the Soviet Union and the United States competed with one another to hasten. This was a task in which sophisticated technology could provide no substitute for more basic political skills. Throughout Africa and Asia, and particularly in Asia, nationalist movements were being stiffened by cadres of Marxists who had learned from Lenin the techniques of revolutionary organization and were to learn from Mao Tse-tung how to combine such organization with guerilla war against an unpopular incumbent government backed by foreign troops.

Mao's techniques had been devised to deal with the Japanese occupation of China between 1937 and 1945, and were perfected in his campaigns against the American-armed forces of Chiang Kai-shek between 1946 and 1949. They were to be imitated with signal success by Ho Chi-minh against the French in Indo-China between 1946 and 1954; but in Malaya and Singapore the British were able, thanks to a combination of patience, political skill, and favourable local circumstances, to defeat them. The French Army determined to learn from their defeat, studied the concept of *la guerre révolutionnaire*, and devised counter-measures which they attempted to put into effect in quelling the insurrection in Algeria which had been threatening ever since 1945. They failed, partly because of the obstinate non-cooperation of the indigenous French inhabitants, partly because the French people made it clear that they were unwilling to support another prolonged colonial war involving sometimes highly unsavoury means, and partly because of the irreconcilable dilemma implied by their slogan, *l'Algérie française*. Algerians were no longer content to be ruled by Frenchmen any more than Indians were prepared to be ruled by the British or, a century earlier, Italians had been prepared indefinitely to tolerate the Austrians. Indigenous governments dependent upon foreign arms, advice, and capital were no better able to find a basis for popular consent; as the Americans were to discover, in their turn, in Vietnam.

So by the last quarter of the twentieth century the horizons of European armed forces had once more shrunk to the defence of their own territorial area—itself, as we have seen, not a simple task. Their problems were to prove as much social and political as military. The armed forces were no longer seen, as they had been for a century and a half, as the embodiment of national pride, the cadre of the nation in arms. The development of technological sophistication which has been traced in the foregoing pages had increasingly made them into technical specialists, relying on weapon power rather than manpower for their effectiveness; and although continental countries retained conscript service as a national institution, the core of the armed forces had to be found from highly-skilled professionals whose services were in demand from other sections of the economy and whom it was not easy either to recruit or to retain.

Moreover the preservation of peace for three decades resulted, as it had after the Napoleonic Wars, in the breeding of a generation uninterested in military affairs, sceptical of the military virtues, and regarding the armed forces with a mixture of suspicion, incomprehension, and contempt. In Germany in particular, whose military traditions had so tarnished a reputation, the armed forces found it difficult to attract the interest and support of the young; but throughout the Western world a generation born in peace and unable to visualize any situation other than peace went to extreme lengths to distance itself from the military by the casualness of its dress, the length of its hair, and its relaxed life style. It seemed so self-evidently preferable to make love, not war. The more politically conscious among them were more keenly aware of the inequities within their own political and social systems and those with which they were involved elsewhere in the world than they were of any dangers threatening them from outside. For many of them, to play any part in defending those systems, especially if it involved participating or acquiescing in the use of weapons of mass destruction, was tantamount to becoming accomplices in perpetrating the injustice committed or tolerated by their governments.

Since the conduct of war in the nuclear age no longer called for masses of reservists trained in military skills and indoctrinated with military attitudes, the dissemination of these attitudes of scepticism, indifference, and hostility has had little immediate impact on the military strength of Western Europe. But in the long run it is bound to make itself felt. It is likely to undermine the self-confidence of the military themselves, and it will strengthen the opposition to the large military budgets which the increasing cost of weapons compel the armed forces to demand. One may feel some gratification that, after a thousand years of armed conflict within Europe, a society has developed which feels itself sufficiently secure to turn its back on the traditional military virtues; but this must be tempered by apprehension that, in a world so heterogeneous and unpredictable as that in which we live, such confidence may prove premature. Nothing has occurred since 1945 to indicate that war, or the threat of it, could not still be an effective instrument of state policy. Against peoples who were not prepared to defend themselves it might be very effective indeed.

Notes

Chapter 1   The Wars of the Knights

1. R. A. BROWN, *The Origins of Modern Europe*, London, 1972, p. 93.
2. See LYNN WHITE, *Medieval Technology and Social Change*, Oxford, 1966, p. 2.
3. J. HUIZINGA, *The Waning of the Middle Ages*, London, 1937, *passim*.
4. M. H. KEEN, *The Laws of War in the late Middle Ages*, London, 1965, p. 154 ff.
5. SIR CHARLES OMAN, *The Art of War in the Middle Ages*, vol. II, London, 1924, p. 145. Even the German historian Hans Delbrück, normally contemptuous of British claims, gives French casualties at 1,283. (*Geschichte der Kriegskunst*, vol. III, Berlin, 1891, pp. 464–473.)
6. OMAN, *op. cit.*, vol. II, p. 384. FERDINAND LOT, *L'Art Militaire et les Armées au moyen age*, Paris, 1946, vol. II, pp. 8–15.

Chapter 2   The Wars of the Mercenaries

1. HONORE BONET, *L'Arbre des Batailles*, ed. G. W. COOPLAND, Liverpool, 1949. First written circa 1382–7, this rapidly became a standard work, passing through numerous MS and printed editions.
2. See the discussion in IAN BROWNLIE, *International Law and the Use of Force by States*, Oxford, 1963, pp. 8–12.
3. *De Jure Belli ac Pacis*, ed. WILLIAM WHEWELL, Cambridge, 1853, vol. I, p. lix.
4. NICCOLO MACHIAVELLI, *The Art of War*, book III, Chapter 7. THOMAS DIGGES; *Four Paradoxes* (1604), quoted in C. H. FIRTH, *Cromwell's Army*, London, 1902, p. 145.
5. MACHIAVELLI, *The Art of War*, book VII, chapter 1.

Chapter 3   The Wars of the Merchants

1. See R. EHRENBERG, *Capital and Finance in the Age of the Renaissance: A Study of the Fuggers and their Connections*, London, 1938, *passim*.
2. K. R. ANDREWS, *Elizabethan Privateering 1585–1603*, Cambridge, 1964, p. 16.
3. C. R. BOXER, *The Dutch Seaborne Empire 1600–1800*, London, 1965, p. 86.

4. See E. H. KOSSMANN, 'The Low Countries' in *The New Cambridge Modern History*, vol. IV, Cambridge, 1970, p. 368.

5. Quoted in HERBERT RICHMOND, *Statesmen and Sea Power*, London, 1964, p. 9.

6. Quoted in C. W. COLE, *Colbert and a Century of French Mercantilism*, New York, 1939, vol. I, p. 343.

7. Quoted in CHARLES WILSON, *Profit and Power*, London, 1957, p. 46.

8. WILSON, *loc. cit.*, p. 107. DR. MAURICE ASHLEY, who is preparing a biography of Monck, is doubtful of the authenticity of this attribution.

9. Both quoted by RICHARD PARES, *War and Trade in the West Indies 1739–63*, Oxford University Press, 1936, pp. 62–3.

10. CHARLES DAVENANT, *Essay upon Ways and Means of Supplying the War*, London, 1695, p. 16. Quoted in EDMOND SILBERNER, *La guerre dans la pensée économique du XVI au XVIII siècle*, Paris, 1939, p. 69.

11. G. N. CLARK, *War and Society in the Seventeenth Century*, Cambridge University Press, 1958.

12. ANDREWS, *Elizabethan Privateering*, p. 171.

13. J. H. PARRY, *The Age of Reconnaissance*, London, 1963, p. 324.

14. J. H. OWEN, *War at Sea under Queen Anne*, Cambridge University Press, 1938, pp. 61–3.

Chapter 4   The Wars of the Professionals

1. This idea has been elaborated by Professor S. E. FINER in his contribution to CHARLES TILLY (ed.), *The Formation of National States in Western Europe*, Princeton, 1975.

2. HANS DELBRUCK, *Geschichte der Kriegskunst*, vol. IV, Berlin, 1920, p. 281.

3. HANS DELBRUCK, *ibid*, p. 280.

4. Both works are translated and printed in T. R. PHILLIPS, ed., *The Roots of Strategy: A Collection of Military Classics*, London, 1943. See pp. 161, 173, 213.

5. COMTE DE GUIBERT, *Essai générale de tactique*, Liege, 1775, I, p. xiii.

Chapter 5   The Wars of the Revolution

1. For an authoritative survey see PETER PARET, *Yorck and the Era of Prussian Military Reform*, Princeton University Press, 1966, pp. 28–48.

2. ROBERT S. QUIMBY, *The Background of Napoleonic Warfare*, Columbia University Press, New York, 1957, p. 296.

3. MARCEL REINHARD, *Le grand Carnot*, Paris, 1950, vol. II, pp. 100–108.

4. JEAN MORVAN, *Le Soldat impérial*, Paris, 1904, vol. I, p. 479 and *passim*.

5. PHILIP HENRY, 5th Earl Stanhope, *Notes of Conversations with the Duke of Wellington, 1831–1851*, London, 1888, p. 81.

6. Quoted in YORCK VON WARTENBERG, *Napoleon as War Lord*, London, 2 vols., 1902, vol. I, p. 38.

7. WILLIAM BLACKSTONE, *Commentary on the Laws of England*, book 1. ch. 13, (4th edn., London, 1777, vol. I, p. 412).

8. E. F. HECKSCHER, *The Continental System*, London, 1922, p. 120.

Chapter 6   The Wars of the Nations

1. CARL VON CLAUSEWITZ, *Vom Kriege*, book VIII, chapter 3.

Chapter 7   The Wars of the Technologists

1. For examples of this see, for the Germans, ERNST JUNGER, *Storm of Steel*, London, 1929; and for the British, GUY CHAPMAN, *A Passionate Prodigality*, London, 1933.

Notes for Further Reading

General

The most comprehensive work on the subject remains Hans Delbrück, *Geschichte der Kriegskunst im Rahmen der politischen Geschichte* (7 vols., Berlin, 1900–36) and it is unfortunate that it has never been translated. The only work in English which approaches it in scholarly value is E. M. Earle, ed., *Makers of Modern Strategy* (Princeton, 1943), which begins only with the Renaissance. Two useful works which cover, as does Delbrück, the development of warfare from antiquity to the twentieth century are O. L. Spaulding, Hoffman Nickerson and J. W. Wright, *Warfare: A Study of Military Methods from the Earliest Times* (London, n.d. but 1925), and, more comprehensively, R. A. Preston, S. F. Wise and H. O. Werner, *Men in Arms: A History of Warfare and its Interrelationships with Western Society* (London, 1956). J. F. C. Fuller, *Decisive Battles of the Western World* (3 vols., London, 1954–6) deals with the subject much more broadly than his title would suggest. On the more recent period J. U. Nef, *War and Human Progress* (London, 1950) is particularly interesting on the connection between economic development and weapon technology; and Theodore Ropp, *War in the Modern World* (Duke University, 1959) provides a first-rate bibliography.

The Wars of the Knights

The framework for the study of warfare in the Middle Ages is provided by Delbrück, *op. cit.*; Sir Charles Oman, *A History of the Art of War in the Middle Ages* (2 vols., London, 1924) and Ferdinand Lot, *L'art militaire et les armées au moyen age* (2 vols., Paris, 1946); but a more concise summary for the earlier part of the period is to be found in John Beeler, *Warfare in Feudal Europe 730–1200* (Cornell University Press, 1971). For the later part, see Edouard Perroy, *The Hundred Years War* (London, 1951), C. T. Allmand, ed., *Society at War: the Experience of England and France during the Hundred Years War* (Edinburgh, 1973) and Philippe Contamine, *Guerre, état et société a la fin du moyen age* (Paris, 1972). On particular aspects see M. H. Keen, *The Laws of War in the late Middle Ages* (London, 1965) and Sidney Toy, *A History of Fortification from 3000 BC to AD 1700* (London, 1955).

The Wars of the Mercenaries

The institution of the mercenaries in general is covered by Fritz Redlich, *The Military Enterpriser and his Work Force* (2 vols., Wiesbaden, 1954) and so far as Italy is concerned by Michael Mallett, *Mercenaries and their Masters: Warfare in Renaissance Italy* (London, 1974). The essay by F. L. Taylor, *The Art of War in Italy 1494–1529* (London, 1921) still remains worth consulting, as does, more generally, Sir Charles Oman, *The Art of War in the Sixteenth Century* (London, 1937). For the economic background of the period see R. Ehrenberg, *Capital and Finance in the Age of the Renaissance* (London, 1938). The chapters by Professor J. R. Hale in the first three volumes of *The New Cambridge Modern History* cover the sixteenth century broadly and definitively. On the later part of the century see especially Geoffrey Parker, *The Army of Flanders and the Spanish Road 1567–1659* (Cambridge, England, 1972).

The Wars of the Merchants

The expansion of Europe in general is well sketched by J. H. Parry in *The Age of Reconnaissance* (London, 1963), and, *Trade and Dominion: the European Overseas Empires in 18th century* (London, 1971). More detail will be found in the same author's *The Spanish Seaborne Empire* (London, 1969); C. R. Boxer, *The Dutch Seaborne Empire 1600–1800* (London, 1965); and, also by C. R. Boxer, *The Portuguese Seaborne Empire* (London, 1969). The development of economic conflict in the seventeenth and eighteenth centuries is traced by Charles Wilson, *Profit and Power: a Study of England and the Dutch Wars* (London, 1957); G. L. Beer, *The Old Colonial System* (2 vols., New York, 1912); G. S. Graham, *Empire of the North Atlantic: the Maritime Struggle for North America* (London & Toronto, 1958); J. H. Owen, *War at Sea under Queen Anne* (London, 1938); and Richard Pares, *War and Trade in the West Indies, 1739–63* (London, 1936). On the economic doctrines behind the conflicts see E. F. Heckscher, *Mercantilism* (2 vols., London, 1935); C. W. Cole, *Colbert and a Century of French Mercantilism* (New York, 1935); and Edmond Silberner, *La guerre dans la pensée économique du XVI au XVIII siécle* (Paris, 1939).

On the development of naval power see Carlo M. Cipolla, *Guns and Sails in the Early Phase of European Expansion 1500–1700* (London, 1965); R. and R. L. Anderson, *The Sailing Ship* (New York, 1967); K. R. Andrews *Elizabethan Privateering 1585–1603* (Cambridge, England, 1964); and, more generally, Michael Lewis, *The Navy of Britain* (London, 1948) and Sir Herbert Richmond, *Statesmen and Sea Power* (London, 1946).

The Wars of the Professionals

Michael Roberts, *Gustavus Adolphus* (2 vols., London, 1958) contains the best account of the development of military ideas in the early seventeenth century. For the development of the French army see Louis André, *Michel le Tellier and Louvois* (Paris, 1942), A. Corvisier, *L'armée française*

de la fin du XVIIe siècle au ministère de Choiseul (2 vols , Paris, 1964), and
E. G. Léonard, *L'armée et ses problèmes au XVIIIe siècle* (Paris, 1958). On the
Prussian army, see Ferdinand Schevill, *The Great Elector* (Chicago, 1948);
F. L. Carsten, *The Origins of Prussia* (London, 1954); and Christopher
Duffy, *The Army of Frederick the Great* (London, 1974). On Britain see
C. H. Firth, *Cromwell's Army* (London, 1902) and C. T. Atkinson, *Marl-
borough and the Rise of the British Army* (London, 1921). On eighteenth-
century warfare in general see Spenser Wilkinson, *The Defense of Piedmont,
1742–1748* (Oxford, 1927) and Robert S. Quimby, *The Background of
Napoleonic Warfare* (New York, 1957). Geoffrey Symcox, *War, Diplomacy
and Imperialism, 1618–1763* (New York & London, 1973) prints some
interesting documents. On the importance of the military in the formation
of European states during this period, see Samuel E. Finer, 'State and
Nation-Building in Europe: the Role of the Military', in Charles Tilly,
ed., *The Formation of National States in Western Europe* (Princeton, 1975).

The Wars of the Revolution

J. L. Colin, *L'Education militaire de Napoléon* (Paris, 1906) and *The
Transformations of War* (London, 1912) give the best short accounts of the
developments in land warfare during this period, which should be
supplemented by Matti Lauerma, *L'artillerie de campagne française pendant
les guerres de la Révolution* (Helsinki, 1956). For Carnot read Marcel
Reinhard, *Le Grand Carnot* (2 vols., Paris, 1950) and for the French
Revolutionary system, Robert R. Palmer, *Twelve who Ruled: the Committee
of Public Safety during the Terror* (Princeton, 1941). On the Napoleonic
period in general see Georges Lefebvre, *Napoléon* (Paris, 1947); on the
Napoleon armies, Jean Morvan, *Le Soldat impérial* (Paris, 1904); on the
Napoleonic campaigns, David Chandler, *The Campaigns of Napoleon*
(London, 1966). On the Prussian army William O. Shanahan, *Prussian
Military Reforms 1786–1813* (New York, 1945) and Peter Paret, *Yorck and
the Era of Prussian Reform* (Princeton, 1966) are comprehensive. The
British army's adjustment is described by Richard Glover, *Peninsular
Preparation: the Reform of the British Army 1795–1809* (Cambridge, 1963)
and Sir Charles Oman, *Wellington's Army* (London, 1912).

For naval warfare see the works of Richmond and Lewis cited for 'The
Wars of the Merchants' above, and G. J. Marcus, *A Naval History of
England*, vol. II (London, 1971). Sir Julian Corbett, *Fighting Instructions
1530–1816* (Navy Records Society, vol. XXIX, London, 1905) provides
important technical detail. On the blockade E. F. Heckscher, *The
Continental System* (London, 1922) remains the standard work. A. T.
Mahan's classic study *The Influence of Sea Power upon the French Revolution
and Empire* (2 vols., London, 1893) contains much of permanent value.

The Wars of the Nations

Cyril Falls, *A Hundred Years of War* (London, 1953) covers the main
points in this period quite admirably, but J. F. C. Fuller, *War and Western*

Civilization 1832–1932 (London, 1932) and Hoffman Nickerson, *The Armed Horde 1793–1939* (New York, 1940) give livelier if more controversial accounts. Colmar von der Goltz, *The Nation in Arms* (London, 1913) is not only factually informative but gives the authentic 'feel' of the period. E. A. Pratt, *The Rise of Rail Power in War and Conquest 1833–1914* (London, 1915) remains the standard work on that subject. On military developments in general see J. Colin, *The Transformation of War*, cited above; Michael Howard, *The Franco-Prussian War* (London, 1961), and the chapter by the same author in vol. XI of *The New Cambridge Modern History*. Walter Goerlitz, *The German General Staff* (London, 1953) is lively and descriptive but more solid studies of the German military are to be found in Gordon Craig, *The Politics of the Prussian Army* (Oxford, 1955) and Gerhard Ritter, *The Sword and the Sceptre*, vols. 1–2 (London, 1972). For the French army see Joseph Monteilhet, *Les Institutions militaires de la France, 1814–1924* (Paris, 1932), Raoul Girardet, *La Société militaire dans la France contemporaine, 1815–1939* (Paris, 1953), and Richard D. Challener, *The French Theory of the Nation in Arms 1866–1939* (New York, 1955). The subject is brought up to date by Pierre de la Gorce, *The French Army* (London, 1963). On the militarism of the period see Alfred Vagts, *A History of Militarism* (London, 1959).

On the First World War see B. H. Liddell Hart, *A History of the First World War* (London, 1970); Marc Ferro, *La Grande Guerre 1914–1918* (Paris, 1969) and, for the economic and social aspects, Frank P. Chambers, *The War Behind the War 1914–1918* (London, 1939). These aspects of both World Wars are summarized by Arthur Marwick, *War and Social Change in the Twentieth Century* (London, 1974).

The Wars of the Technologists

For naval warfare see the works of Lewis and Richmond cited above, together with James P. Baxter, *The Introduction of the Ironclad Warship* (Cambridge, Mass., 1933) and Bernard Brodie, *Sea Power in the Machine Age* (Princeton, 1941). Douhet's doctrines of command of the air are to be found in Giulio Douhet, *Command of the Air* (London, 1943), and the importance of similar ideas in the Royal Air Force are described, with their results, in Sir Charles Webster and A. N. Frankland, *The Strategic Air Offensive Against Germany* (4 vols., London, 1961). The development of ideas about mechanized warfare are discussed with remarkable objectivity by B. H. Liddell Hart in the first volume of *The Tanks: the History of the Royal Tank Regiment* (2 vols., London, 1959). On the general problems of formulating defence policy between the wars see D. C. Watt, *Too Serious a Business: European Armed Forces and the Approach to the Second World War* (London, 1975). The Second World War itself is most comprehensively and objectively covered by Peter Calvocoressi and Guy Wint, *Total War* (London, 1972), and, more briefly, by A. J. P. Taylor, *The Second World War* (London, 1975).

The Nuclear Age

For brief and authoritative surveys of events since 1945 see Alastair Buchan, *War in Modern Society* (London, 1966) and Bernard Brodie, *Strategy in the Missile Age* (Princteon, 1959), but both concentrate very largely on the problems of nuclear warfare. On revolutionary wars in the Third World, G. Bonnet, *Les Guerres insurrectionnelles et révolutionnaires* (Paris, 1958) and Otto Heilbronn, *Partisan Warfare* (London, 1962) provide useful historical introductions. A good general analytic approach is to be found in Carl Leiden and Karl M. Schmitt, *The Politics of Violence: Revolution in the Modern World* (Englewood Cliffs, N. J., 1968), and a comprehensive study in Lawrence Martin, *Arms and Strategy: An International Survey of Modern Defence* (London, 1973).

Index

Index

Abercrombie, Sir Ralph, 89
Aerial warfare, in World War I, 127;
and resolution of war, 128–9; as a
deterrent, 129; belief in power of
bombing attacks, 130; defence
against, 130; *blitzkrieg* strategic
concept, 132; and the civilian, 134;
alleged dominance of battlefield,
138
Africa, exploration, 52, 121;
nationalism, 141
Aircraft, submarine-hunters, 127;
reconnaissance tasks, 127, 128; jet
propelled, 135
Albania, *stradiots*, 77
Alexander I of Russia, 92
Algeria, rebellion against France, 141
Amadis de Gaul, 16
America, army, in Revolutionary
Wars, 78, 89
see also United States
American Civil War, use of railways,
98; the cavalry, 104; *Merrimac/
Monitor* encounter, 123
Amiens, Peace of, 1802, 90–1
Angevins, 8, 10
Anjou, House of, and throne of
Naples, 20
Antwerp, Spanish Fury 1574, 29
Aragon, House of, and throne of
Naples, 20
Archers, archery, cross-bow, 8, 31;
long-bow, 11, 32; lethalness of
arrows, 11; at Crécy and Agin-
court, 12, 14
Ariosto, Ludovico, 16
Armed forces, professional, 54; main-
tenance in peace-time, 55; and
drilling, 55, 56; concept of dis-

cipline, 56, 121; conscription, 58;
instruments of a single controlling
will, 59–60; officials for their control and development, 62–4;
bureaucratic backing, 64–6;
officer-corps, 69–70, 107–8; rigid
hierarchical structure, 70; problems of movement and provision-
ing, 71; vocabulary, 71; long time
at peace, 72; and strategic developments, 77; waging of *la Grande
Guerre*, 95; military schools, 95;
source of national safety, 99–100;
demand for larger forces, 105;
demands of modern troops, 107;
as embodiment of the Nation, 110,
141–2; and political power, 114–
15; need for versatility, 122, 134;
sink to territorial defence, 141–2;
become technical specialists, 142
Armies, 20; French pattern, 24–5;
return expected from investment,
27; attraction for adventurous and
poor, 28; and social status, 28–9;
search for unplundered territories,
37; expense compared with navies,
49; self-contained universe with
own subculture, 72; isolation from
rest of community, 72–3, 94;
increased speed and flexibility, 76,
77; free-moving, free-firing skir-
mishers, 76, 77; need for specialist
leadership, 77; use of *guerre des
postes*, 77, 78; reorganization on
Napoleonic pattern, 83–4; revert
to eighteenth century pattern, 94;
need for government and community resources, 99; limitations
imposed by supply problems, 99,